THE CREDIT CARD *TRAP!*
WHAT YOU DON'T KNOW
<u>*WILL*</u> *COST YOU*

Robert M. Benedict

 **PUBLISHING**

Valrico, Florida

The information in this book provides a general overview of financial principles and topics. Since government regulations change and every family situation is different, this book is not intended to take the place of consultation with a financial expert when specific legal, tax accounting or investment guidance is needed.

THE CREDIT CARD *TRAP!*
WHAT YOU DON'T KNOW <u>WILL</u> COST YOU

Copyright © 2010 Robert M. Benedict

BNS Publishing
Valrico, FL 33596

www.thecreditcardtrap.com

ISBN 978-0-9779544-14

Library of Congress Control Number: 2010905266

TABLE OF CONTENTS

I want to give special thanks to the many people who provided input and encouragement on the manuscript and development of this book.

My deepest thanks to each for the time and insight provided:

Eric Benedict
Jason Benedict
Steve Brown
Robb Hiller
Pam Hiller
Deb Krieg
Jeanne McCanna
Michael McCanna
Tom McCanna
Kim Meyer
BreAnn Rumsch
Joel Rumsch
Charles Schroeder
Pamela Schroeder

Thanks also to my wife, Pauline, for the word processing of the multiple manuscript drafts and for her understanding during my hours of research and writing.

Cover Art: Steve Pavlicek
Cover and Book Design: Mike Lundborg

PART 1

SLAVERY IN
THE 21ST CENTURY

The rich rules over the poor,
and the borrower is the
slave of the lender.

Proverbs 22:7 RSV

SLAVERY IN THE 21ST CENTURY

Most Americans believe that slavery ended in the 19th century. The idea that one human being could legally subject another human being to often cruel practices, as they destroy their personal freedom – creates a sense of outrage in most of us.

Yet slavery does exist today in the 21st century. There is one country in particular (whose name I will later reveal), that has legalized it and shamelessly promotes it for the economic gain of its businesses. The ones who are victimized into slavery are often young and/or uninformed of the trap they are being lured into.

I have been to that country – and I have met one of the slaves. I will call her Hannah to protect her privacy.

There are hundreds of thousands like her, if not millions. Hannah is no longer a statistic to me. She is a real human being – like you and me. She pleaded with me to share her story with as many people as possible. It may not help Hannah, but it may help many others like her who have been victimized. That is her desire – and mine.

A Business Trip

I was on a business trip that brought me to Hannah's city. She waited tables at the hotel restaurant where I was staying. As she introduced herself and told what was available on the menu, it was apparent she was well educated and spoke fluent English.

At first, I estimated her age as early twenties – but the dark circles under her eyes and the halting manner in which she walked, suggested she was older. As she turned to take my order to the kitchen, I was shocked to see shackles on her ankles, connected by a small chain. Yet no other guest expressed surprise. It was as if it were as commonplace as the sun rising in the east and setting in the west.

On my first two visits, Hannah had many guests to wait on, so our conversation consisted of no more than quick pleasantries as she took my order.

On my third visit, however, there was virtually no one else in the cavernous eating area. Hannah was much more relaxed as she took my order. She asked what I was doing in her city and I explained that I taught negotiating seminars for purchasing and sales professionals in companies around the world.

I wasn't sure she understood, but she smiled and nodded politely as I spoke. When I asked her story, she glanced from side to side, then nervously told me her story in a half whisper.

HANNAH'S STORY

She said she was a slave to a cruel master, who forced her to pay him virtually all her meager earnings. She worked long hours at two separate jobs – usually 7 days a week. Her neck, back and feet were almost always in pain – some days more intense than others. She was provided with much strong coffee to help her overcome her constant sleep deficit.

Hannah said her only hope for freedom was to pay back everything she owed to her master and that would take many, many years.

When I asked how she had become a slave, she assured me that it had not always been this way.

According to Hannah, she had a very happy childhood, raised by loving, middle-class parents who sacrificed much to help her get a good education. She and her friends enjoyed their childhood very much, laughing and playing and dreaming about what their lives would be like when they grew up.

They dreamed of going to the University and getting good paying jobs and making a contribution to their world that would help others and make their lives significant. They visualized themselves as having enough money to wear beautiful clothes, eat at the finest restaurants, attend glittering theater presentations, enjoy exciting sporting events and travel to exotic spots around the world.

As loving and giving as her parents were, Hannah also dreamed of the day she would leave home and experience total freedom. Then she would decide for herself what she did – and when she did it. She would go where she wanted to go and do what she wanted to do. Most of all, she would have the freedom to make her dreams come true.

To her delight, and her parent's absolute joy, Hannah was accepted at the University when she was 17 years old. She was absolutely convinced that she was now on her way to absolute freedom and the path to seeing her dreams become reality.

However, it was during her first year at the University that the deception occurred, resulting in the destruction of not only her dreams – but her personal freedom.

The Deception

During a beautiful spring day on campus, Hannah was introduced to the most distinguished and handsome man she had ever met. His clothes were impeccable, well-tailored and meticulously pressed. His watch and rings were obviously very expensive.

Not a hair was out of place and his deeply tanned face revealed dazzling white teeth and a winning smile.

He was surrounded by a crowd of students who hung on his every word – and laughed often at his jokes. He was so confident and his manner so winning that she felt spell-bound as she listened to him.

"Now there's a man who can make anyone's dream come true," a friend said to her.

Just then, the man pointed to a nearby vendor and said to the group, "Ah, my friends, it's time for coffee and pastries. You are indeed my friends and I will pay for it all. You deserve it!"

As the crowd quickly moved to the vendor's kiosk for free refreshments, amazingly the man came over and introduced himself to Hannah, and invited her to join him at his table for coffee.

According to Hannah, he quickly set her at ease and, after exchanging pleasantries, he asked about her dreams for the future. He was as good a listener as he was a speaker. He was so attentive that she felt like there was no one else in the whole world but the two of them.

She found herself excitedly telling him every dream in detail: The beautiful clothes she would one day wear, the wonderful theater and sporting events she would one day attend, the exotic places she would one day travel to, and the exciting parties she would one day hold for her childhood and college friends.

When Hannah finally finished, the man sat silent for a moment. Then he reached across the table, took her hands in his, looked deeply into her eyes and said, "Hannah, you don't have to wait. Those dreams can come true now, beginning today."

She was stunned, unable to comprehend what he was saying.

"How?!" she heard herself say. "I have no money. I'm just a student."

"Hannah, Hannah," he said in a fatherly manner, with a knowing smile coming kindly across his face. "I have a great deal of money and love nothing more than to help people realize their greatest dreams."

When she asked him what she would have to do, he said, "We'll make an agreement. You realize your dreams now, when you're young and can still enjoy them to the fullest. Then pay me back later."

With that he took out the biggest roll of money she had ever seen and peeled off ten bills. "Go buy yourself that dress you dreamed of. There is also enough for matching shoes, purse and jewelry."

Peeling off one more bill, he added, "And here is enough for theater tickets for you and a friend."

"Just like that?" she asked. "That's all I have to do?"

Reaching into the inside pocket of his expensive silk suit, he brought out a piece of paper. "All you need to do is sign this little form."

As she picked it up to read it, he laughed and said, "It's just a bunch of legal jargon that says you received the money and will pay me with a bit of interest for using it. That's fair, isn't it, Hannah? A little interest in exchange for your dreams coming true? Enjoy now, pay later!"

He was right. It was a lot of legal jargon that was virtually incomprehensible. It sounded too good to be true, but she so much wanted it to be true. "How do I know I can trust you?" she asked. Her boldness surprised him – and her.

He quickly composed himself, then presented the most disarming, kindly smile. "Hannah, look around you at all of these people. Almost all of them have the same agreement with me. They trust me."

She looked at the crowd of happy, laughing people, feasting on free coffee and pastries, given by this obviously wealthy and generous man. If they are all doing the same thing to have dreams come true – why not her? Enjoy now, pay later.

"I'm sorry. I didn't mean to offend you earlier," she said shyly.

"You did not offend me, Hannah. You only increased my respect for you. You are an intelligent young woman, with a mind that must have answers."

With that, he handed her the pen and she signed the agreement and took the money. The man gave her a fatherly hug and announced to the others,

"Hannah is making the first of her many dreams come true. Let's give her a hand."

They all cheered and applauded. One of them shouted, "Now that you have money, you're going to know what real freedom is like."

According to Hannah, those words were wonderfully accurate in describing the next few months of her life. Rather than going home for the summer, her life became a whirlwind of parties with her friends, exciting sporting events, dazzling theater performances, beautiful clothes of every type, sumptuous meals at the finest restaurants in the city and even travel to far away places she had read about as a child.

Whenever she had a need for more money, she would go to her friend. He never said no. He would smile broadly and say, "Of course, Hannah. You deserve to have your dreams come true while you're young. Enjoy now. Pay me later."

He would have her sign a little form and then hand her whatever money she asked for. She was so grateful in her young heart toward this kind, generous man. She was thinking about him one day as she sat at the very coffee kiosk where she had first talked to him. As she looked up, over her coffee cup, she saw him coming toward her with a man in a uniform next to him.

Gratitude toward him so overwhelmed her that she ran to him and threw her arms around him.

The Trap Closes

According to Hannah, he brusquely took her arms off his neck. With great anger in his voice, he demanded that she immediately pay everything that was owed him – pointing to a fist full of notes that she had signed.

She was so taken back, at first she thought he was joking. He said if she didn't pay the notes and interest immediately that he would turn her over to the police.

Hot tears rolled down her face as she pleaded with him. "You told me I could pay later."

"Later has arrived. Later is now," he retorted with a cold cruelty in his eyes she had not seen before – not even thought possible.

When she said she couldn't pay, the policeman immediately shackled her wrists and told her she could either go to jail or be enslaved to her "friend," who would now be her master.

"My world fell apart," Hannah said to me as she wiped the tears from her face. "I was no longer in charge of my life. He now directed everything I did. No college. No friends. Only work. I was now a slave serving a master – and a very cruel one at that."

She said her parents tried to help, but the interest rate on what she owed was so great that the amount was far beyond their means to pay.

"Is it legal to charge those kinds of rates?" I asked.

"Very legal indeed," she said sadly. "It was not always this way. For many years our government protected us against these practices that lead to slavery. But then greed entered in and certain businesses are very influential in the councils of our government."

She paused for a moment and said, "And I, too, bear responsibility. I should never have agreed to something I didn't understand. And I should have known it was too good to be true. I was young and I was foolish. But what a terrible price to pay," she said, pointing to her shackles.

Just then three men dressed as gardeners, and three women dressed as maids entered the restaurant. Hannah momentarily left to pour each of them one glass of water. As they turned to leave, I noticed that they too were shackled.

16

Hannah returned to my table and said, "Those were some of the students who were with me the day I met the man who was going to make all of our dreams come true; the one who gave us free coffee and pastries; the one who laughed and joked with us at the kiosk and told us we didn't have to wait to make our dreams come true and to experience real freedom."

Then she told me the obvious. "They too are slaves. Virtually all of their earnings go to the master. There is now little joking or laughter. Freedom is a distant memory."

She sighed deeply and stood up to leave.

"What can I do?" I asked.

"You can tell others. You can warn them. You can tell my story in the hope that others will be wiser and not fall into their trap. I say their trap, because it is not just one man that does this. There are many men and many women involved in the enslavement industry – and they are well trained to prey upon the young and uninformed. They have enslaved millions, destroying their freedom and ruining their lives.

Tears streamed down her face as she asked me to tell her story to as many people as I could – in the hope that her story would help save others.

That is Hannah's desire – and that is mine.

Revealing The Country

And now I will reveal the name of the country where Hannah lives – the one that has legalized slavery and refuses to change its laws and practices that cruelly destroys the freedom of so many of the young and uninformed citizens – for the obscene profits of the greedy.

It is the United States of America.

Before You Toss This Book Down...

Before you toss this book down saying that slavery doesn't exist in the United States and that it certainly isn't legal – I'd ask you to consider that:

- Slavery comes in many forms
- Shackles are not always made of metal

Let me also quickly add that:

Hannah Is A Real Person who I met on a business trip to St. Louis, MO. Though I have taken some artistic license in how I related it, the essence of her story is absolutely true.

She did, indeed, work long, long hours at two minimum wage jobs – 7 days a week.

She did, indeed, experience constant sleep deficit and severe neck, back and foot pain – while paying a cruel master who took virtually all of her meager earnings.

She did, indeed, plead with me to tell her story to young people and the uninformed about the terrors of financial slavery – so they could avoid her bondage.

The Master In The Story Is Really The Credit Card Industry, who targets the young and uninformed, luring them with "free prizes, low introductory rates" and the enticement of "buy now...pay later."

Later, they close the trap, throwing borrowers into overwhelming interest rates of 16, 22, 25 – even 35%!

How does the trap close? According to an award-winning program produced by FRONTLINE® and *The New York Times*, often in the most insidious ways:

The following is from the introduction to that program:

> In 'Secret History of the Credit Card,' FRONTLINE® and *The New York Times* joined forces to investigate an industry <u>few Americans fully understand.</u> In this one-hour report, correspondent Lowell Bergman uncovered the techniques used by the industry to earn record profits and get consumers to take on more debt...

The program goes on to detail those specific techniques.

> According to Harvard Law Professor Elizabeth Warren, the credit card companies are misleading consumers and making up their own rules. "These guys have figured out the best way to compete is to put a smiley face in your commercials, a low introductory rate, and hire a team of MBA's to lay traps in the fine print."

> Warren and other critics say that a growing share of the industry's revenues come from what they call deceptive tactics, such as "default" terms spelled out in the fine print of cardholder agreements – the terms and conditions of which can be changed at any time for any reason with 15 days' notice.

> <u>Penalty fees and rates are sometimes triggered by just a single lapse</u> – a payment that arrives a couple of days or even hours late, a charge that exceeds the credit line by a few dollars, or a loan from another creditor which renders the cardholder "overextended" as defined

by the nation's three all-powerful credit bureaus. This flurry of unexpected fees and rate hikes come just when consumers can least afford them.

Banks are raising interest rates, adding new fees, making the due date for your payment a holiday or a Sunday in the hopes that maybe you'll trip up and get a payment in late, says Robert McKinley, founder and chairman of Cardweb.com and Ram Research, a payment card research firm. It's become a very anti-consumer marketplace.

How can credit card companies get away with these tactics and rates?

How can credit card companies legally do these things? According to the FRONTLINE®/*The New York Times* program, it's because the banking industry successfully eliminated a critical restriction: The limit on the interest rate a lender can charge a borrower.

In the interview with FRONTLINE®, Elizabeth Warren summarized it this way:

> What's changed is that when credit was deregulated in the early 1980's, the contracts began to shift. And what happens is that the big issuers, the credit card companies who have the team of lawyers, started writing contracts that effectively said, "Here are some of the terms, and the rest of the terms will be whatever we want them to be." And so they would loan to someone at 9.9% interest. That's what it said on the front of the envelope. But it was 9.9% interest... unless you applied for a couple of other credit cards, or 9.9% interest unless you defaulted

on some other obligation somewhere else that doesn't cost me a nickel. And at that moment, that 9.9% interest credit suddenly morphs to 24.9% interest, 29.9% interest, 36.9% interest.

Nobody signs contracts to buy things that say, "I'm going to pay you $1,200 for the big-screen TV unless you decide, in another month or two months, that it should really be $3,600 or $4,200 or $4,800." But that's precisely how credit card contracts are written today.

Complaints about these types of practices were so widespread that after decades of brutal abuse, the US Congress acted to curb at least some of them. I commend the Congress – this was a significant step forward (to see a summary of the Credit Card Act of 2009, see Appendix #1).

As I'll delve into later, there was no such thing as the credit card industry policing itself. Even though there were outcries across the country about their practices being highly unethical, deceptive and enslaving of numerous people and families – the credit card masters refused to change.

It took Congress outlawing some of these predatory practices and providing for severe penalties to finally get their attention. This is the "nature of the beast." This is the cruel character of "the master."

However, Congress did NOT deal with the greatest underlying method of enslavement that these companies have unleashed on the young and uninformed – *the enormous rates of interest!* Until that is dealt with, financial slavery will still be alive, well, and legal in the United States.

Financial Slavery Was Legalized In The United States In 1978 And Confirmed In 1980

In the story you just read, I asked Hannah if it was legal in her country to charge the kind of interest rates that enslaved her.

"Very legal indeed," she said sadly. "It was not always this way. For many years our government protected us against these practices that lead to slavery. But then greed entered in, and certain businesses are very influential in the councils of our government."

Her statement is true indeed about the United States. For most of our nation's history, rates of 16-35% interest were illegal – and people who charged them went to jail. It was called loan sharking or predatory lending, and was carried out by only the most unsavory characters in our society, who preyed upon the helpless and the uninformed.

The reason the government established usury laws to protect its citizens, was that it understood the explosive and dangerous power of high interest rates to overwhelm and destroy a borrower – in essence, committing them to very real economic slavery.

Up to 1978, nearly all states had usury laws limiting rates to between 6-12%.

A Supreme Court ruling in 1978 and a law passed by Congress in 1980 destroyed the states' protective laws and introduced economic slavery into the United States.

Bankrate.com columnist, Leslie McFadden, provides a history of this in her March 11, 2009 article:

The 1978 Supreme Court decision Marquette National Bank vs. 1st of Omaha Service Corp. concluded that national banks, such as Bank of America and Citibank, can charge the highest interest rate allowed in the bank's home state – regardless of where the borrower lives. This means that credit card issuers located in states with liberal or non-existent usury laws, such as Delaware and South Dakota, can "export" the lack of an interest rate cap to customers in states with usury laws in place.

Next, section 521 of the Depository Institution's Deregulation and Monetary Control Act of 1980 gave state chartered banks the same rate-exporting powers. The law allows all federally insured banks, including state charted banks, to charge out of state customers the highest interest rate permissible in the state, territory or district where the bank is headquartered.

Practically speaking, it was the end of state usury laws. It was the beginning of the legalization of interest rates that had sent people to jail for most of the nation's history.

Lucy Lazarony, columnist with Bankrate.com, in an article called, "Credit Card Companies Side Step Usury Laws" states, "For hundreds of years, societies all over the world have protected borrowers by limiting interest rates charged by lenders. But in today's credit card market, American borrowers are on their own."

I want to briefly outline in the next section why these formerly criminal interest rates of 16-35% were outlawed for so many years.

COMPOUNDING INTEREST IS THE GREATEST ECONOMIC FORCE ON THE FACE OF THE EARTH

Years ago, a nationally known TV talk show host quipped, "The defense department announced it has found something more powerful than nuclear weapons and far more efficient. It actually leaves all buildings intact, while completely destroying the people inside. It's called 17% interest."

When the talk show host quipped that 17% interest was stronger than an atomic weapon and destroyed people while leaving the property untouched, he had no idea that credit card rates would one day be at 18, 22, 25 – even 35% interest.

Albert Einstein declared compound interest the most powerful force in the universe and also called it the eighth wonder of the world.

Here's a classic example of how powerful compounding interest can be:

Would you rather have $1 million or one penny that doubled in value every day for 30 days?

VALUE OF ONE PENNY DOUBLED
EACH DAY FOR 30 DAYS

PERIOD	BALANCE	PERIOD	BALANCE
Day 1	$0.01	Day 16	$327.68
Day 2	$0.02	Day 17	$655.36
Day 3	$0.04	Day 18	$1,310.72
Day 4	$0.08	Day 19	$2,621.44
Day 5	$0.16	Day 20	$5,242.88
Day 6	$0.32	Day 21	$10,485.76
Day 7	$0.64	Day 22	$20,971.52
Day 8	$1.28	Day 23	$41,943.04
Day 9	$2.56	Day 24	$83,886.08
Day 10	$5.12	Day 25	$167,772.16
Day 11	$10.24	Day 26	$335,544.32
Day 12	$20.48	Day 27	$671,088.64
Day 13	$40.96	Day 28	$1,342,177.28
Day 14	$81.92	Day 29	$2,684.354.56
Day 15	$163.84	Day 30	$5,368,709.12

As you can tell by the chart above, if you had said you wanted the $1 million, you would have missed out on over $4 million!

> **Compounding interest is a wonderful friend and ally to those who use its power on their behalf through saving. However, it is an unmerciful enemy to those who are in high interest debt.**

What is compound interest? Here are two definitions:

"Interest earned not only on an original investment, but on its accrued earnings as well." (www.cbtfinancial.com)

"A method of computing interest based on a geometric formula which accrues interest with increasing rapidity as time passes." (www.retirementadvisor.ca)

Here are sobering examples of compounding interest rates working against a person who is in debt:

- The amount owed on money borrowed at 8% doubles in 10 years.
- The amount owed on money borrowed at 16% doubles between the 4th and 5th year.
- The amount owed on money borrowed at 25% doubles between the 3rd and 4th year.
- The amount owed on money borrowed at 35% doubles between the 2nd and 3rd year.

What credit card interest rate are you paying?

CAN YOU IMAGINE OPENING THE
NEWSPAPER AND SEEING A
HEADLINE THAT READS...

𝔇𝔞𝔦𝔩𝔶 𝔑𝔢𝔴𝔰

Tuesday, April 6

SPECIAL SALE!

EVERYTHING IS NOW PRICED AT DOUBLE ITS NORMAL PRICE!

For 3 days only, absolutely every item in our inventory will be available for twice its standard price.

You would probably scratch your head and say, "That must be a misprint." Or you would say, "That's absolutely crazy. Someone would have to be insane to do that." But every time someone uses a credit card at these rates and only pays the minimum payment – they are paying double, triple or quadruple the original price, depending on the number of years they continue to only pay that minimum payment!

When compounding interest is unleashed against a person or family at these rates, it is like a tidal wave.

Unfortunately, uninformed people have little idea of the force they are up against when they approve the legal jargon on the incomprehensible credit card form. They think that if they pay the minimum payment, things will eventually be fine – and they are so wrong!

Information is Power

So here's information that the powerful masters in the credit card industry don't want you to have. It emphasizes again the crushing power of compounding interest at these astronomical rates:

CREDIT CARD RATES AT 16%

If your credit card is at 16% and you only pay the minimum payment your card requires (usually 2.5% of the total owed – so $250 on a $10,000 balance), how long will it take you to pay off your balance?

Answer: 24 years and 10 months – and that's if you never add to the balance again.

If we take $10,000 owed as the balance example, you would have paid $21,005.93 to pay off the debt – or $11,005.93 in interest.

IN OTHER WORDS, YOU WOULD HAVE PAID DOUBLE FOR EVERY PURCHASE YOU MADE WITH THAT CARD. Think about that... you would have paid double for every meal, tank of gas, article of clothing, movie ticket, vacation, laptop – everything you bought with that credit card!

Let's say, however, you doubled your minimum payment ($500 on a $10,000 balance). How long will it take you to pay off your debt?

Answer: 2 years

That is a savings of nearly 23 years!

What about smaller balances, like $1,000? Is it still advantageous to pay more than the minimum?

If your credit card is at 16% and you only pay the minimum payment your card requires (usually 2.5% of the total owed – so $25 on a $1,000 balance), how long will it take you to pay off your balance?

Answer: 8.5 years and that is if you never add to the balance again.

Let's say, however, you doubled your minimum payment to $50 on a $1,000 balance. How long will it take you pay off your debt?

Answer: 2 years.

Even on this small balance, doubling the minimum payment (and continuing to pay that amount even when the minimum required goes down), will save 6.5 years of payments

CREDIT CARD RATES AT 25%

If your credit card is at 25% and you only pay the minimum payment your card requires (usually 2.5% of the total owed – so $250 on a $10,000 balance), how long will it take you to pay off your balance?

Answer: 63.5 years – and that's if you never add to the balance again.

If we take $10,000 owed as the balance example, you would have paid $47,703.14 to pay off the debt – or $37,703.14 in interest.

IN OTHER WORDS, YOU WOULD HAVE PAID NEARLY 5 TIMES OVER FOR EVERY PURCHASE YOU MADE WITH THAT CARD.

Let's say, however, you doubled your minimum payment ($500 on a $10,000 balance). How long will it take you to pay off your debt?

Answer: 2 years and 3 months.

That is a savings of over 60 years!

What about a $1,000 credit balance?

If your credit card is at 25% and you only pay the minimum payment your card requires (usually 2.5% of the total owed – so $25 on a $1,000 balance), how long will it take you to pay off your balance?

Answer: 17.5 years and that is if you never add to the balance again.

Let's say, however, you doubled your minimum payment to $50 on a $1,000 balance. How long will it take you pay off your debt?

Answer: 2 years and 3 months.

Even on this small balance, doubling the minimum payment and continuing to pay that amount even when the minimum required goes down, will save nearly 15 years of payments.

Do you see the amazing power of compounding interest at work here?

Do you sense how stunningly its exponential power increases as the rates go up?

Wait until you see the figures for the next rate!

CREDIT CARD RATES AT 34%

Unfortunately, there are a significant amount of people at this overwhelming and crushing rate.

If your credit card rate is at 34% and you only pay the minimum payment your card requires, how long will it take you to pay off your balance (The credit card calculator topped out at 34% and 2.5% minimum payment will never retire the debt. So, at 3% or $300/month for a $10,000 balance)?

Answer: 178.6 years – by the way, that's 2 lifetimes and that is if you never add to the balance again.

If we take $10,000 owed as the balance example, you would have paid $175,034.42 to pay off the debt – or $165,034.42 in interest.

IN OTHER WORDS, YOU WOULD HAVE PAID APPROXIMATELY 16 TIMES OVER FOR EVERY PURCHASE YOU MADE WITH THAT CARD.

On this example, let's say you didn't even double the payment, but kept the same $500 on a $10,000 balance, how long will it take you to pay off your debt?

Answer: 2.5 years.

That is a savings of over 176 years!

If we take $10,000 owed as the balance example, you would have paid $14,953.02 to pay off the debt – or $4,953.02 in interest. That's a savings of $160,081.40 in interest.

Why the enormous difference between a 16% credit card rate and a 34% credit card rate? Why aren't those figures approximately double rather than so astronomically different?

Answer: The explosive, exponential, enslaving power of compound interest working against you!

Truth That Can Help Set You Free

For three decades, consumer groups begged the credit card industry to provide this type of information to card holders. The industry refused and fought every legislative effort that compelled them.

Why? Information is Power! They feared that if borrowers understood, they would pay far more than the minimum and reduce their debt. That is exactly what the credit card masters did not want.

It literally took an act of Congress in 2009 to finally force credit card companies to inform consumers about this – 30 years after the financial slavery laws were passed in the US, and compounding interest at formerly criminal rates were unleashed on the American people.

Now, they will have to reveal on the statement how long it will take to pay off the balance if you just pay the minimum payment. They will also have to reveal what it will take to pay off the current balance in 3 years. Look for these figures and pay attention to them!

Masters don't want slaves to be free. That's why Hannah wants her story to be told. Maybe there are people who will hear it, understand it, and avoid the economic slavery that destroyed her freedom and dreams.

This Is Not Just Hannah's Story – It's The Story Of Millions Of People

As Hannah said, "You can tell my story in the hope that others will be wiser and not fall into their trap. I say their trap because it is not just one man that does this. There are many men and women involved in the enslavement industry – and they are well trained to prey upon the young and uninformed.

"They have enslaved millions, destroying their freedom and ruining their lives."

How true her words are.

90 Million Americans Carry Credit Card Debt

According to the FRONTLINE® and *New York Times* report referenced earlier, in 2004, 90 million Americans carried an average of $8,000 in credit card debt from month-to-month (as opposed to 55 million who paid off their credit card balances in full each month).

After stating that the credit card industry calls people who pay their monthly balances on time "deadbeats," the report goes on to say:

> The industry's most profitable customers, the ones being sought by creative marketing tactics, are the "revolvers," the Americans who carry monthly credit card debt.

Ed Yingling, incoming president of the American Bankers Association, tells FRONTLINE® that revolvers are "the sweet spot" of the banking industry. This "sweet spot" continues to grow as the average credit card debt among American households has more than doubled over the past decade. Today, the average family owes roughly $8,000 on their credit cards. This debt has helped generate record profits for the credit card industry – last year, more than $30 billion before taxes.

The Impact of Compounding Interest

Credit card companies understand the enormous power of compounding interest – *and they are using it to generate enormous profits.*

Millions of Americans lack understanding about compounding credit card interest. It is often said: *"What we don't know won't hurt us."* That's not true as it applies to the overwhelming power of this financial force.

What we don't know does hurt us. In the Bible, God says, "My people perish for lack of understanding." God was applying this to many areas, but it certainly strongly applies to this area of finance.

Compounding interest working for you over time will produce wealth. Compounding interest working against you over time can absolutely destroy your finances and your future. In fact, many marriage counselors say that debt and fights over finances are the most frequent causes of divorce.

According to an interview with Elizabeth Warren (quoted earlier), the author of several books, including "The Two Income Trap: Why Middle Class Mothers and Fathers Are Going Broke:"

> 70% of American families last year said that they are carrying so much debt that it is making their family lives unhappy. Middle-class Americans, hard working, play-by-the-rules Americans, Americans who lost a job, who don't have health insurance, who are in the middle of a divorce – those are the Americans who are carrying enormous credit card debt.

Credit Card Debt is Growing – Quickly!

A November 20, 2005 *ABC News* original report titled, "Americans Slammed by Credit Card Debt," stated that the average debt owed on credit cards had climbed from the $8,000 figure in 2004 to $9,000 in 2005:

> For all their convenience, credit cards can cause a lot of damage: Most Americans have credit card debt, and the average American owes more than $9,000 to credit card companies.

By May of 2006, the figure had grown to nearly $9,500.

> Americans now owe about $800 billion on credit cards – up from $273 billion in 1992. In fact, US households with at least one credit card carried an average of $9,498 in credit card debt, nearly twice the level of a decade ago. (*ABC News*, Feb. 1, 2007)

At the end of 2008, the *Associated Press* reported that www. creditcard.com, found the average outstanding US credit card debt per household was $10,679.

Credit Card Debt Tops $1 Trillion!

As of 2009, debt owed by Americans on credit cards topped $1 trillion – with the majority on cards that had rates of 16-35%.

What will the average debt owed on credit cards be at the time you are reading this? I don't know, but one thing seems to be sure – it will be substantially more UNLESS WE DECIDE TO DO SOMETHING ABOUT IT.

The Battle For The Future – Our Young People Targeted

The *ABC News* original report referenced earlier stated:

> Americans often are drawn into such a dilemma by tantalizing solicitations. Promises of low interest rates and low monthly payments will pop on to the computer screen or arrive in the mail.
>
> It can be hard to resist, especially for younger consumers like college students.
>
> "There have been desks with credit card vendors," said one college student, Chrisson Jon Taylor. "It happens fairly regularly – also at the dorm site, moving in. You know, they get you as soon as you get here."
>
> Frequent shopping sprees got college student Rebecca Mahl into a lot of trouble.

"As long as I kept putting a little bit towards it, I thought I'd be OK," she said. "But it just kept building up and it was overwhelming."

Please notice Rebecca's comment: *"It just kept building up and it was overwhelming."* That's the underlying, relentless power of compounding interest working against her. Like with Hannah in my earlier example, it enslaved her before she understood what was even happening.

The credit card industry is targeting the young and the uninformed.

Here is the sobering concluding sentence to the *ABC News* report:

It's a habit that begins in college and affects people for the rest of their lives.

WHAT CAN BE DONE?

Start with the young and all those who do not have credit cards. Let them know the truth and the truth will keep them free.

Hannah believed that if her story was told and the truth revealed about the credit card trap, many young people could avoid the financial slavery she experienced.

She believed that if people understood the awesome power of compounding interest at 16-35%, they could withstand the allure of low interest rates, free prizes, and the temptation of "buy now, pay later."

Here is Hannah's plea and the rest of her story:

> Credit cards are not 'tickets to freedom' – they are
> "passports to slavery." Unless you can pay the balance
> in full every month, avoid them at all costs.

When I wrote Hannah's story, it was written as an allegory. Make no mistake, however, her story is indeed real – and so is she. In her actual situation, she signed up for a credit card on her first day of freshman orientation at college. There were 10 brightly colored booths on campus with credit card representatives offering food, beverages, prizes and low introductory rates.

The booth where Hannah signed up had a huge sign over it that read: *MAKE YOUR DREAMS COME TRUE!*

As she turned in the application to the handsome, well dressed credit card representative, who had been so persuasive and listened so attentively to her dreams about the future, he said, "Hannah, when your card arrives in the mail, remember that your dreams are just one swipe of the card away from coming true. Your credit card is your ticket to freedom."

Hannah told me she quickly found out that her credit card was NOT a ticket to freedom; it was a passport to slavery.

As she said in the story, "And I, too, bear responsibility. I should never have agreed to something I didn't understand. I should have known it was too good to be true. I was young and foolish... but what a terrible price to pay."

Within 6 months of getting her credit card, Hannah was working 20 hours every weekend at a minimum wage job – just to pay the ever growing minimum payment. Even though she stopped using the card, the 35% interest rate and late fees kept exploding the principle. Despite the fact that she paid virtually every dime of her earnings to the "credit card master," she wasn't making a dent in the overall total that she owed.

Within one year of getting her card, she had dropped out of college and was working one full-time, minimum wage job Monday through Friday – *and* her part time job 20 hours every weekend. Aside from paying basic survival living expenses, every available dime went to pay off her debt to the master.

When I met her at the hotel restaurant and she waited on my table, I can tell you that the dark circles of fatigue under her eyes were very real – as was the pain in her neck, back and feet from working 7 days per week. Many times she walked with great difficulty despite being in her early 20's. Her shackles were not made of metal, but they were just as real.

I conducted seminars on negotiations about six times a year in St. Louis. Each time I would stay at the same hotel. Each time I would seek out Hannah to find out her new, decreasing balance. Then, I would congratulate and encourage her on her progress.

If I was assigned a different waitress, Hannah would stop by my table with an update and a look of pride on her face. She would also ask if I had told her story to anyone who would be helped by it.

After a long, long time, the day finally arrived when she made the last payment on her debt. Smiling brightly, she sauntered over to my table. "You are looking at a free woman," she said. "My debt has been paid and I am free."

"I feel like the slaves must have felt when they were set free."

"I used to tell people that at least I had a chance to enjoy the fun times running up the debt. I will never say that again. The fun did not compare in any way with the pain I went through to pay it off."

"But now I am free. I am free indeed and I will never be a slave to debt again!"

While I long ago lost contact with Hannah, I will never forget her courage and her determination to "pay the price" to be set free – and what her story could mean to others who hear it.

Your Help is Needed

The credit card industry is targeting our young people with millions of dollars worth of advertising because they understand that the battle for the future will be won by shaping the attitudes of this group. So do we.

The Credit Card Trap – An International Challenge

While this book focuses primarily on the United States, the credit card companies are targeting the young and uninformed in countries worldwide. There are a number of countries in Europe and Asia who are deeply alarmed at how many of their people are in severe credit card debt – and how quickly it is growing.

How do you counteract millions of dollars of advertising?

One person, one family, one friend at a time.

Your help is urgently needed. Would you please share Hannah's story with the young people you know who will soon be going off to college, vocational school, or entering the work force? Would you share your knowledge about the enormous power of 16-35% compounding interest and the slavery it can bring?

Then, ask them to share Hannah's story with as many of their friends as possible. Texting, Twittering, e-mails, Facebook, blogging and countless other methods enable our young people to get the message out quickly.

If possible, encourage them to take a seminar by such financial experts as Dave Ramsey (www.DaveRamsey.com), Ron Blue (www.ronblue.com), or Crown Financial Ministries (www. crown.org). In fact, go with them if you can.

Getting a firm financial footing for our young people is vital for their future, the future of their families, and the future of America. You can make a difference one person at a time.

A Great Beginning, But Don't Stop!

Your help to young people is where we need to start – but not stop. There is a country that needs your help. It is a country that has gone from being the largest creditor nation in the world loaning freely to other countries and giving to many nations, to the largest debtor nation in the world. This happened in just three decades. It is... the United States of America.

The Urgent Need For An American Economic Revolution

In a few short decades, America has gone from being a nation of savers, whose savings fueled the strongest economy in the world – to a nation of debtors, enslaved with a trillion dollars worth of credit card debt exploding at the largest interest rates in our nation's history. This is at a time that the big banks are borrowing from the US government at historic low interest rates. As a result, in 2009, their profits were a record $55 billion.[1] The big banks understand compounding interest – and they continue to unleash it on the American people at unparalleled credit card rates.

Our government owes other nations vast amounts of money and our economy has shrunk beyond recognition – recently teetering on the brink of collapse.

If ever we needed to make revolutionary changes in the way we handle finances – it's now!

Some revolutions are created by the young, some by the more experienced. This revolution will need both groups.

What's next?

Part 2 will provide 15 Freedom Weapons and 7 specific steps to help you break free from credit card debt – or, if you are not in credit card debt, to speed you on your way to financial freedom.

A number of unique tools will be introduced to help capture savings and increase motivation, as you transform the greatest financial force on earth (compounding interest) from an unmerciful, enslaving enemy to a powerful ally and friend.

Debt does not have to be a way of life. It is not your destiny!

Even though 90 million Americans are carrying credit card debt and 85 million are living paycheck-to-paycheck without savings – know that you were created to live in freedom as a saver and a giver, not a debtor and a slave.

If you are ready – it can happen!

Want to substantially reduce your credit card rate?

If your current credit card is with a big bank and your rate is between 16-35%, you may be able to immediately and substantially reduce your rate by moving your balance to a:

- Credit union
- Small community bank

Unlike banks, credit unions actually do have a national usury law that caps their interest rates at 18% – though most are well below that.

A Pew Study in October 2009 analyzed the twelve largest banks and the twelve largest credit unions. Not surprisingly, they found that the credit unions advertised rates of 9.9-13.75% were far lower than those of the big banks.

I recently mentioned this to a young man whose bank credit card company raised his rate to 26%, despite his paying his bills on time and having excellent credit.

He went straight to his credit union and was immediately approved at 10%! Needless to say, he moved his entire credit card balances from two bank cards to the credit union and saved himself 16% in interest rate!

That is the impact of a national usury law that caps interest rates.

Another example is from the *Huffington Post*,[2] "Measuring the Move." Commenting on new credit union member, Michael Wingate, it said:

"Michael was shocked when his Citibank credit card rate jumped from 4.99% to 40.99%! He has a stable job as a supervisor at an aircraft parts manufacturing company. His credit score is good, over 700. He made his payment to Citibank on time.

"The CEO of Generations Credit Union, Marylin Ball-Brown, whose credit union is participating in the American Debt Relief Challenge, said it was the highest credit card interest rate she had ever seen. In the 1980's the rate would have been considered usury. It is an example of the difference between for-profit banks and not-for-profit credit unions.

"The credit union saved the family $33,000 over the life of the credit card by transferring the $10,400 Citibank card balance to an unsecured loan with a traditional rate of 12.2%."

This again is the impact of a national usury law that caps interest rates.

Commenting further on the Pew Study:

"The study also found penalties to be less frequent and less severe for both interest rates and fees at credit unions. Nearly half of all credit unions surveyed did not impose penalty rates on their credit cards, while 90% of banks did. And since credit unions must stay below their 18% usury cap, the penalty rates maxed out there, while banks charged a penalty rate of 28.99%."[3]

The time you spend researching this may save you hundreds of dollars per month in interest – money that could help achieve your key goal: Break Free From All Credit Card Debt.

For more information about how to join a credit union and/or how to contact a credit union or small community bank near you, go to Appendix #2.

---

[1] Feb. 24, 2010, AP article titled, "Wall Street Bonuses Top $20 billion," by Michael Gormley.

[2] Feb. 1, 2010 article titled, "Measuring the Move," *Huffington Post.*

[3] FRONTLINE'S®, *The Card Game,* a Q&A on credit unions.

PART 2

AN AMERICAN ECONOMIC REVOLUTION FROM THE GRASS ROOTS UP

*One person, one family,
one friend at a time.*

RECOMMENDATION #1
SIGN YOUR OWN DECLARATION OF INDEPENDENCE
FROM CREDIT CARD DEBT – AND GO TO
WAR TO ACHIEVE IT!

RECOMMENDATION #2
ESTABLISH A FREEDOM ACCOUNT – TRANSFORM
YOUR FINANCES AS YOU CHANGE AMERICA

RECOMMENDATION #3
ESTABLISH A GOD Account – TRANSFORM YOUR LIFE
AS YOU CHANGE THE WORLD

AN AMERICAN ECONOMIC REVOLUTION
FROM THE GRASS ROOTS UP

The following three recommendations could potentially revolutionize the way millions of families approach their finances, help re-shape America and positively impact the world.

RECOMMENDATION #1 –
SIGN YOUR OWN DECLARATION OF
INDEPENDENCE FROM CREDIT CARD DEBT –
AND GO TO WAR TO ACHIEVE IT!

If you are one of the 90 million credit card holders who carries a balance on your credit card, I am going to ask you to do something that is absolutely revolutionary in America today.

I am going to ask you to sign your own personal Declaration of Independence from credit card debt – and go to war to achieve it!

There is a far better way than carrying credit card balances at 16-35% interest to buy what you need or dream of having. It's called paying cash – and there are many specific ideas (Freedom Weapons) in the pages ahead to show how.

When you buy something with cash, you pay for it once – not 2, 5, or 16 times due to astronomical interest rates working against you.

There is also a far better way than carrying credit card debt of 16-35% interest to pay for emergency car repairs, house repairs or medical bills.

It's called a Freedom Account (recommendation #2) and you pay for those emergency items only once – not 2, 5, or 16 times.

By doing this, you pocket those savings on your way to financial freedom.

Already Enslaved?

What if you are like Hannah and aren't just carrying a credit card balance, but are enslaved by the ever growing debt? Hannah's plea and example to you would be, "Make it the passion of your life to break free!"

What that meant for Hannah and will mean for you is:

- Do whatever it takes to STOP using your "passports to slavery."

  If you are digging yourself into a hole, stop digging! If you are going the wrong way, you need to turn around! Like the colonists in America did when they knew they had to break free from England, they declared their independence with a vision of freedom – and then went to war to win it. You are involved in a war with compound interest – the greatest economic force on earth.

The next section will provide 15 Freedom Weapons to help you accomplish this.

- Pay DOUBLE your monthly minimum payment on your credit cards – and keep paying that figure even when the monthly minimum goes down. As we discussed in Part 1, this practice will get you free amazingly more quickly than just paying the minimum.

- Pay your credit card bill the day it arrives to guard against outrageous late fees and getting bumped into an even more enslaving interest rate.

STORE CREDIT CARDS

"Would you like to save 10% on your purchase today?"

The enslavement from credit card debt doesn't only occur through VISA, MasterCard, Discover and American Express, it also includes store cards that can carry exceedingly high interest rates.

The next time a store salesperson says: *"Would you like to save 10% on your purchase today by getting our store's credit card?"* Remember, most stores are not trying to save you anything. They want you in debt paying for their merchandise many times over – through brutal interest rates!

DO I NEED A CREDIT CARD TO BUILD MY CREDIT RATING?

No. You can build your credit score by:

- Paying your bills early
- Paying more than the minimum required
- Taking out a loan for the amount of cash you have on hand and then paying the loan back early

AM I AGAINST CREDIT CARDS?

No. I am against credit card <u>debt</u> – especially at enslaving interest rates.

If you can pay the bill in full each month and live within your means, credit cards are useful. However, if you know from past experience that you can't pay them off in full each month – cut them up, melt them down, and destroy them before they destroy you.

Life Without Credit Cards?

There was a time, not so long ago, when few Americans had credit cards – and we lived very well. We were a nation of savers with one of the highest savings rates in the world. Our surplus capital enabled our economy to expand and be the strongest in the world. We were the #1 country that loaned to other nations – and we also gave generously in foreign aid.

Today, the United States is the largest debtor nation on the face of the earth, begging other nations to buy our treasury notes of debt to prop up our shaky economy – even as we mortgage our future.

In an article on the opinion page of the *Pittsburgh Tribune-Review,* Nov. 17, 2009, a Chinese immigrant named Yeh Lingling, asked a question for all of us to consider: "The United States went from being the world's top creditor nation to being the world's greatest debtor nation in less than three decades. What happened?"

While there are many reasons, one is that our vision defining the "American Way of Life" got radically changed.

In our period of great economic strength (as families and as a nation), here were some of the maxims we knew to be true and practiced:

- Save now, buy later
- If you don't have the money for something, don't buy it
- Short term pain for long term gain
- Debt is serious and to be paid off ASAP
- Savings are essential; they bring financial freedom

During the last three decades, when credit card companies got massive interest rates made legal, and lured millions of Americans into their enslaving system through vast expenditures on advertising, the maxims we lived by got reversed.

- Buy now, pay later (at 2, 5 of 16 times what was originally paid)
- If you don't have the money, buy it anyway (you deserve it)
- Short term gain for long term pain (which we are now experiencing)
- Debt is a way of life (that doesn't have to be true)
- Savings aren't important (how can you attain financial freedom with no savings?)

So, how are the above principles working out for us as individuals, families and a nation? Obviously, not well. The results have been devastating.

Had enough? Are you, your family, and friends ready for revolutionary change? Is debt-ridden America ready for a return to our earlier financial concepts:

- Save now, buy later
- If you don't have the money for something, don't buy it
- Short term pain for long term gain
- Credit card debt brings slavery, savings bring freedom

Why Have a Declaration of Independence?

We need to re-establish the correct and clear vision for ourselves, our families and our nation – one that leads to economic freedom, not slavery.

In its colonial system, Great Britain forced the colonies to buy manufactured goods from the mother country at high prices. Loans were limited to British banks at very high interest rates. The American colonists claimed that these practices amounted to economic slavery – and they were right!

There were many other abuses detailed in the nation's Declaration of Independence. For instance, there was taxation without representation – in other words, it was a one-sided agreement. The master (King and Parliament) dictated what they wanted and the economically enslaved Americans had no say. It was a one-sided agreement (not unlike today's credit card agreements).

Up until just a few years before the Revolutionary War started, the majority of American colonists understood the abuses – but according to historians, certainly didn't believe America could successfully break free of Great Britain. After all, the British had the most powerful army and navy in the world. They were the most powerful military force on earth (just like compounding interest is the most powerful economic force on earth).

Most Americans felt that things were what they were – they couldn't change. The idea that the American colonies would ever be the United States of America – free from the abuses, including economic slavery, would have been regarded as... well, revolutionary (kind of like believing that today's Americans could ever be free of enslaving credit card debt – or that 90 million Americans might seriously consider never again using their credit cards).

As the abuses continued, public opinion began to change one person, one family, one friend at a time. Clearly, this was aided by newspaper articles, books, pamphlets, sermons, and public speeches – as well as neighbors who talked with one another "over the fence," at taverns, church and community gatherings.

After the Continental Congress tried repeatedly and unsuccessfully to address the abuses and reconcile with Great Britain – they finally had enough. They codified their grievances in the Declaration of Independence and declared themselves free and independent. It provided to the people of the colonies a vision that unified them.

As individuals, families, and a nation, we need to see a vision of ourselves as savers and givers who are financially free and independent – not as debtors and slaves who believe that debt is a way of life. If we can't see the vision of being free of enslaving credit card debt, we will never be free. You cannot achieve a goal that you cannot see.

The Bible says, "where there is no vision, the people perish." The vision always precedes the actualization, just like a blueprint precedes the construction of a building.

That was the role of the Declaration. It was a unifying vision that was distributed by the hundreds of thousands of copies.

Were the Americans immediately free upon the signing of the Declaration? By no means! It took a war with much sacrifice to bring freedom. Your war with your debt will require sacrifice to bring freedom as well – and so will America's.

Are You Ready?

Have you had enough? Are you ready to declare your independence from credit card debt? Are you willing to live by the principles that guided our families and nation to prosperity just a few decades ago?

Would you please go to our website at www.thecreditcardtrap. com and sign a copy of the Declaration of Independence from credit card debt? Would you be willing to be a part of an American economic revolution from the grass roots up?

Like McDonalds proudly displays their ever increasing number of hamburgers sold, we'd like to display the ever increasing number of Americans who have declared their independence from credit card slavery – and are willing to go to war to achieve their freedom.

Would you be willing to share a copy of the Declaration and/or this book with your friends in conversations "over the fence," at work, church, community organizations, etc?

By the way, not only does your family need for you to win this war – America needs for you to win.

THE DECLARATION OF INDEPENDENCE FROM CREDIT CARD DEBT

When in the course of human events, it becomes necessary for one person to dissolve the economic bonds that have enslaved them to another – and to assume, here on the earth, the rightful position that nature and nature's God intended:

To live as a saver and a giver,
Not a debtor and a slave

We hold these truths to be self evident: That all men and women are created equal. That they are endowed by their Creator with certain inalienable rights – that among these are life, liberty and the pursuit of happiness.

Having seen the ravages of credit card debt on millions of our fellow countrymen, we also hold these truths to be self evident: That while debt may bring short term happiness, its long term impact is economic slavery rather than liberty, economic death rather than life – and sadness, anxiety and depression rather than happiness.

I now declare that I am no longer willing to pursue short term happiness for long term enslavement.

I will make it one of the primary passions of my life to break free from all credit card debt on my way to living my life debt free – as a saver and a giver, not a debtor and a slave.

SIGNATURE   DATE

RECOMMENDATION #2
ESTABLISH A FREEDOM ACCOUNT – TRANSFORM YOUR FINANCES AS YOU CHANGE AMERICA

Tens of millions of Americans live "paycheck to paycheck." What that means is that millions of families have no savings to meet the unpleasant surprise of an unexpected car repair, house repair or medical expense.

An article in Careerbuilders.com titled, "Majority of US workers Live Paycheck to Paycheck," stated, "More than six in ten (61%) of US workers live paycheck to paycheck to make ends meet." This was according to a survey conducted by Harris Interactive during the period May 22 to June 10, 2009.

The article also said that this 61% figure was a significant rise over a 49% figure in 2008.

So, when an unexpected $700 car repair hits, or the washer or dryer need to be replaced for $500, or a medical bill arrives for $900, what do many of these paycheck to paycheck Americans do? They pay it with a credit card at 16-35% interest – because they wrongfully feel they have no alternative.

One can almost hear the clinking of the chains and feel the chafing of the shackles as they go even deeper into economic slavery.

According to the Bureau of Labor Statistics, there were approximately 140 million people employed in the US at the end of 2009. 61% of that total would be about 85 million people living without savings.

THE FREEDOM ACCOUNT

The Freedom Account is a special, dedicated savings account that is only used for emergencies – such as the ones just mentioned. It is not to be used for day to day purchases.

My grandparents and parents called it their Rainy Day Account. My wife and I called ours the Cushion Against Chaos account. Many financial counselors call it the Emergency Fund. In all cases, it is the same concept: Money set aside to deal with the unexpected.

When unpleasant surprises occur – there is no chaos or plunge into economic slavery by using a credit card. The individual or family:

- Simply uses the money in their Freedom Account and pays cash!
- Replaces the cash ASAP by the same methods they used to establish it.
- Pays no interest, because they borrowed from themselves. They were their own bankers!

How Much Money Should be in the Freedom Account?

Most financial counselors would recommend three levels:

- First level – $1,000
- Second level – equivalent to three months of your take home salary
- Third level – six months of your take home salary

At the time of this writing, the average American makes about $2,500/month take-home pay. So, the second level for the average American would be about $7,500 in a Freedom Account. The third level would be approximately $15,000 (for people over 45).

If you find yourself in disbelief that you can do this, remember that you live in a society that has programmed you to believe that way. Others have done it and you can too! It is the beginning, the foundation of escape from financial bondage and entrance to financial freedom.

Should I Save for the Freedom Account First or Start Paying off my Debt First?

Establish the Freedom Account first. Otherwise, when an emergency hits, you will have no option other than more credit card debt at 16-35%. Save the first $1,000 – then go after your credit card debt.

HOW TO CREATE A FREEDOM ACCOUNT

There are only two ways to do this and they both require sacrifice:

1. Increase Income
2. Decrease expenses

Remember, this is nothing less than a war for your financial freedom (as well as America's). As with any war, it will require sacrifice, planning and on-going motivation to win.

Here are some weapons that can help:

 FREEDOM WEAPON #1 – Turn Your Trash into Treasures

Do an inventory of things you own and no longer use – and sell these on e-bay or Craigslist, garage sales or consignment shops.

I have talked to people who have successfully sold boats, furniture, antiques, jewelry, exercise equipment, fishing and hunting gear, tools, dishes – even old cars and gained two advantages. First, the items were no longer gathering dust as they took up space. Secondly, they were converted into cash for the Freedom Account.

I have talked to students who have sold bicycles, games, old text books, and electronics they no longer use (as well as clothes they never wear to consignment shops) and used the funds to build their Freedom Account.

FREEDOM WEAPON #2 – Part Time Job

Some people have taken part time jobs delivering newspapers or pizza, mowing lawns or shoveling snow, working at a car wash, as a waitress/waiter, or as a greeter at Wal-Mart. They have put every penny into the Freedom Account to put themselves on a firm financial footing.

FREEDOM WEAPON #3 – Pack Your Own Lunch

Estimated Savings: $100-$200 monthly. $1,200-$2,400 annually

Many working Americans eat lunch away from home, sometimes at a company cafeteria, sometimes a fast food restaurant, sometimes at a more upscale establishment. Most people would agree they could, on average, save $5 per day by packing their own lunch from home. Doing this five days per week would save $25 per week or $100 per month. This practice alone would get the individual to the $1,000 level by the tenth month. If there are two working adults in the family, following the same practice, the $1,000 level would be reached by the end of the fifth month.

How to capture the savings:

Each day that a meal is packed, put $5 into a glass jar that sits conspicuously on the kitchen table (where you will see it many times during the day). Then, bank the total at the end of the week into your Freedom Account.

In addition, establish a thermometer on the refrigerator where it can clearly be seen. Track the progress toward the $1000 goal by filling in the various amounts with a magic marker each week (hint – make it a big thermometer so each bit of progress looks substantial).

The more visual you can be the better! It's a tremendous way to keep the goal constantly in front of you and stay motivated. Out of sight, out of mind – in sight, in mind!

By the way, your children and friends who visit will definitely ask what the Freedom Thermometer and Freedom Jar are about. It will be a great opportunity to increase the impact of the revolution from the grass roots up – one person, one family, one friend at a time.

Freedom Thermometer & Freedom Jar

Note: If you are uncomfortable with having actual cash in the Freedom Jar, or rarely use cash, you can substitute "play money" (like in the Monopoly game) or make up paper IOU's. At the end of the week, add these up and make your deposit in your Freedom Account.

FREEDOM WEAPON #4 – Capturing Loose Change

Estimated Savings: $150-$600 annually

If you have ever consistently put your pocket change into a jar or drawer, you have probably been stunned when you brought it to the bank. Over time, those forgettable pennies, nickels, dimes and quarters mounted up to $50, $60 or $70!

It is estimated that over the course of a year, that an individual or husband and wife can capture between $150-$600 just by consistently putting their loose change in a container and periodically bringing it to the bank.

For my wife's parents, consistently collecting their pocket change was how they financed their infrequent but memorable vacations – debt free.

For my parents, it was one of the ways they paid for Christmas – debt free.

Both families clearly understood that little things, done consistently, over time have an enormous impact.

How to capture the savings:

At the end of each day, when you empty the change from your pockets or purse, put it in the Freedom Jar – then deposit it at the end of the week into the Freedom Account. Be sure to track the progress on your thermometer.

For some people who rarely use cash, this idea will have little benefit. But for those who do, this small – but mighty – idea can have significant impact.

FREEDOM WEAPON #5 – When eating in restaurants, order ice water rather than soda or iced tea

Estimated savings: $10/week per person or $40/week for a family of four. $520 annually per person or $2,080 annually for a family of four

The cost of a non-alcoholic beverage at a fast food restaurant averages about $1.50 + $.10 sales tax = $1.60.

In a more formal restaurant, where a waiter or waitress is serving you, the cost averages about $2.25 plus tax and tip. $2.25 + 7% tax + 15% tip (or more) = $2.75.

Since most people eat at both types of restaurants, let's say that the average cost of a soft drink or iced tea is $2 per drink.

Average American eats 5 meals weekly at restaurants

In a January 6, 2009 article in *USA Today* by Nancy Hellmich, titled "Americans aren't running from restaurants," she states, "If you are like the average American, you eat about 5 meals outside your home each week – either take out or dining out. That's according to the NDP Group, a leading market research firm."

So, let's look at the savings achieved by drinking ice water rather than soda or iced tea.

Savings by an individual drinking ice water:

5 meals/week x $2.00 for soft drinks or iced tea = $10/week
$10/week x 4 weeks = $40/month
$10/week x 52 weeks = $520/year

Savings by a family of four drinking ice water:

Let's multiply those individual savings for a family of four.

$10/week savings x 4 people = $40/week
$40/week x 4 people = $160/month
$40/week x 52 weeks = $2,080/year

That's a $2,000+ annual savings just because a family of four decided to drink ice water rather than soda or iced tea!

Little things, done consistently, over time, will have a huge impact.

How to capture the savings:

Each time you return home from eating at a restaurant where you had free ice water rather than soda or iced tea, drop $2 into the Freedom Jar. Have each person in the family that had ice water do the same. At week's end, deposit your Freedom Jar funds and mark the progress on your Freedom Thermometer.

What a teaching tool this is for children when you explain to them what you are doing. Most will not like giving up the sodas at the beginning – but they will like feeling that they are part of the effort.

They will never forget putting the dollars into the Freedom Jar and marking the progress on the thermometer.

Also, this practice will provide a real "forum for discussion" about debt, savings, values, sacrificing for a goal, family, etc.

FREEDOM WEAPON #6 – Make using coupons from newspapers, magazines and the internet a way of life

Estimated savings: $10-$20 weekly. $520-$1,040 annually

Like collecting loose change and turning it into hundreds of dollars a year, using coupons for items you are going to buy anyway can provide hundreds of dollars in savings annually – if not thousands!

In this high tech world we live in, coupon clipping has exploded beyond newspapers and magazines and onto the internet at such sites as www.coupon.com. At these sites, coupons can be downloaded for food, non-prescription drugs, diapers, paper products, auto parts, car rentals, hotels, tires, restaurants and many others.

According to the *Los Angeles Times* business section article, titled: "Coupons are Being Used at a Faster Clip," December 10, 2009, "At coupons.com, one of the first and largest online coupon sites, consumers printed coupons worth $313 million in 2008. The site surpassed that full-year figure in June 2009 and expects $1 billion in printed coupon savings by year's end."

The problem for some people is that a $.50, $1, or $2 food coupon doesn't seem worth the time. However, like collecting pennies, nickels, dimes and quarters, they add up to significant amounts over time. And, in non-food items, the coupons can be quite large. Recently, coupons were $10-$15 on car batteries, and $100-$150 on the purchase of four tires. There were also coupons for a 50% discount on hotel rooms, as well as two free days on a 7-day car rental. These are just a few examples.

During a 12-week financial planning seminar at our church, the general consensus was that a family of four could save $10-$20/week on their $150 food bill alone.

Never buy an item just because you have a coupon! However, if it is something you intend to buy anyway, coupons can be a smart way to capture significant savings.

How to capture the savings:

Look at your grocery receipt or non-food receipts that lists the amount you saved on coupons and immediately deposit that amount of cash into your Freedom Jar upon your return home. At week's end, deposit your Freedom Jar funds and mark the progress on your Freedom Thermometer.

 FREEDOM WEAPON #7 – Limiting Visits to Starbucks, Caribou, or other coffee shops

Estimated savings: $0-$25/person weekly. $0-$1,300/person annually.

If you don't frequent coffee shops, don't spend another moment on this Freedom Weapon #7. But if you do, this could be a powerful weapon for you.

I love Chai Tea lattes at Starbucks and Caribou coffee shops. My wife loves the vanilla coffee latte.

We love to go together – and we love to go separately. Sometimes we add a pastry and we thoroughly enjoy it! At the time of this writing, the cost of the tea or coffee is approx. $4.25 with tax and about $2 for the pastry.

A while back, my wife and I sat down to pay the credit card bill, which we always pay in full. To my surprise, we were averaging five times per week for that period! Let's say that we didn't buy a pastry every time and that the average stop was $5 per wonderful visit.

5x/week x $5.00 = $25/week

If we had done that consistently for a year:

52 weeks x $25 = $1,300/person or $2,600 for us both!

Little things done consistently have a huge impact!

Our solution was:

- We cut back. We just didn't realize how much we were doing. One time per week was a treat, five times per week was an addiction (pleasant, but an addiction none the less).
- We bought Chai Tea at the supermarket. A box that makes four cups costs $4, $1 per cup compared to $4 per cup when purchased at the coffee shop.

On subsequent weekly visits to these wonderfully alluring coffee shops (we even enjoy the aroma of the coffees when we first enter), I did some informal research with both customers and employees.

In particular, when I went first thing in the morning, I met a number of "regulars" who said they literally had lattes 365 days per year – and on some days, they had two!

Employees knew many customers by name and confirmed that not only were there a number of 365-day-per-year customers, but husbands and wives were both every day regulars – and some who also brought their children!

$5/day x 365 days/year = $1,825/individual or $3,650/couple

Again, little things done consistently over time can have a huge impact.

I am not saying not to go to Starbucks or Caribou, but there can be huge savings in cutting it back if you are a regular. Track how many times you stop at a coffee shop per week or pay close attention to your next credit card bill.

How to capture the savings:

Here's a quick approach:

- Estimate how many times you frequent a coffee shop per week
- Decide how many times you (and/or spouse) will cut back
- On the day you deposit into your Freedom Account, multiply the times you did not go x $5 and deposit that amount. Then, track the progress on your Freedom Thermometer.

 FREEDOM WEAPON #8 – Shop rates for your car insurance and get all discounts possible

Estimated savings: $250-$400 per car annually

I invite you to read the following statements from Philip Reed, Sr. Consumer Advice Editor @ Edmonds.com:

> There is a very good chance that you are – this very moment – paying too much for your car insurance. There is an even better chance that you could get a better rate, from another insurance company, than you could from your existing insurer.
>
> So why not take an hour or so and review your policy for potential savings?

The internet has created increasing competition between car insurance companies. It is easier than ever for consumers to shop for low insurance rates, to analyze coverage and compare premiums.

Only compare the best rated companies who will truly pay if you have an accident. However, even as the top companies point out in their TV ads, there is a wide variance in insurance rates.

Go to the search engines on the web and compare. Then compare annually. Sometimes insurance rates will have great rates one year and then raise them substantially the next.

DISCOUNTS: In addition to shopping around, you can usually also get better rates if you:

- Insure all your cars with one company. Usually you can save substantially with "multi-car" discounts, so you should generally insure all your cars in one place if at all possible
- Insure your home and car with the same company. Many companies offer discounts if you have both your home (or apartment) insurance and auto insurance with them. Sometimes you can also get discounts for insuring boats.
- Install an anti-theft unit. Some insurance will provide discounts of up to 36% depending on the category of the anti-theft device.

Sometimes just informing your present car insurance agent that you are shopping rates can cause them to find ways to save you significant money. Also, when you are comparing policies, make sure it's "apples to apples" – the same coverage, deductibles, etc.

How to capture the savings:

When you pay the reduced amount for your new insurance (or the reduced amount you negotiated with your current insurer), immediately write a check for the amount you saved and deposit it into your Freedom Account. Then, track the progress on your Freedom Thermometer. Do this each time you pay your insurance bill.

 FREEDOM WEAPON #9 – Eliminate 1 meal per week at a "sit down" restaurant (The Freedom Meal!)

Estimated savings: $10/person/week = $520/person/year
$40/week for a family of four = $2,080 annually

How many times per week does your family eat dinner at a "sit down" restaurant such as Chili's, Applebee's, Ruby Tuesday, etc. It is challenging for a family of four to have their evening meal at a restaurant for less than $60 when tax and tip are included (especially if there is an appetizer).

Here is a powerful idea that has helped many families: Do one less dinner out per week than you normally do. Research this for yourself. The same meal that you eat at a restaurant can be prepared at home for 1/3 the price. If the average you spend at a non-fast food restaurant for your family is $60, you can prepare it at home for $20 – and save $40/week.

$40/week x 52 weeks = $2,080/year!

Little things done consistently over time can have a huge impact.

I am not asking you to stop eating at restaurants and prepare every meal at home – just eliminate one meal per week at a "sit down" restaurant.

Make the Freedom Meal Special and Memorable

Make this a special evening. If the kids are old enough, maybe let them make the meal. Or, perhaps each person has different duties as a part of preparing it. Other alternatives to make it special might include: music playing during the meal, board games or card games after the meal – or perhaps eating by candlelight.

Maybe it's the same night each week and is consistently pizza night (from a frozen pizza or make your own) or taco night with tacos made from scratch.

How to capture the savings:

At the conclusion of the meal, deposit $10 per person cash into the Freedom Jar and record the progress on the Freedom Thermometer. Make sure the children understand what is happening. This is a teachable moment regarding debt and savings.

 FREEDOM WEAPON #10 – Cut back on the cable TV package and pay-per-view TV

Estimated Savings: $45/month = $540 annually

According to a May 26, 2008 *NY Times* article, entitled "The Ever Rising Cost of Cable," the average monthly revenue for each cable vision subscriber was $75.

Basic packages for most companies in most parts of the country are approximately $30/month. Cable may be an important part of your family's recreational dollars – or, it may be that the difference between the basic package and what you are paying could be a significant area of savings.

In addition, renting DVD's for a dollar at Walgreen's or McDonald's is less expensive than most pay-per-view movies.

In fact, some families have decided that cable TV is not for them and are saving the entire amount.

How to capture the savings:

If you move from a high dollar package to a basic package, track the savings. When you pay your monthly cable bill, immediately put the difference in your Freedom Jar – each month! Then, record the progress on the Freedom Thermometer and deposit it into your Freedom Account.

 FREEDOM WEAPON #11 – Forego the Purchase of Junk Food at the Grocery Store

Estimated Savings: $22.50/week or $90/month = $1,080 annually

At the time of this writing, the average American family of four spends approximately $150 per week on groceries. Of this figure, 25% of the total is spent on what nutritionists would call empty calories or junk food. These are foods that are high in refined white sugar, fats and salt. They include, but are not limited to, potato chips, cheese curls, pretzels, cookies, pies, cakes, ice cream, soda, etc. These are the types of foods blamed by nutritionists for Americans being overweight. Here is an idea that has saved families significant money while making them healthy as well.

Reduce the total percent of the grocery bill spent on empty calories from 25% to 10%. Let's calculate what a 15% savings would equal:

$150/week grocery bill x 15% savings = $22.50/week

PRACTICALLY, HOW DO YOU DO THIS?

- NEVER go to the grocery store when you are hungry.

- ALWAYS make a list before you go – and stick to it! This eliminates a huge amount of impulse buying.

- Be alert! When you go down the aisles that are loaded with snacks, pastries and sodas – THINK! Don't absentmindedly throw packages into your cart. Do the same with ice creams and frozen desserts. Remember that these are the targeted items where your greatest savings come from.

- When you are standing in line at the check-out counter, DON'T automatically throw in candy, gum, newspapers and magazines. There is a reason why stores place these at the check-out area. Guard your savings!

- Don't buy foods at convenience stores such as gas stations or drug stores. They are indeed convenient, but very expensive. They are also havens of junk food.

Does Freedom Weapon #11 take a little effort and planning? Yes, but it will quickly become a habit – a very lucrative and healthy habit for your family. Again, I'm not saying to never eat empty calories – just realize they are expensive, unhealthy and need to be reduced.

How to capture the savings:

If you follow the above guidelines, you can safely assume that most people will save 15% of the grocery bill. Each time you return from the supermarket, look at the total and calculate 15%. Put this amount into your Freedom Jar. Bank the total at the end of the week into your Freedom Account. Track the progress on your thermometer by filling in the appropriate levels with a magic marker.

FREEDOM WEAPON #12 – If you have both a cell phone and land line –consider eliminating the land line

Estimated Savings = $50/month – $600 annually

At the time of this writing, 20% of Americans have cell phones and no land line. The percentage of Americans eliminating their land line(s) and exclusively using their cell phones is growing quickly. Others are using VOIP for local and long distance calls to dramatically cut costs.

There are definitely pros and cons, but it can provide significant savings with minimum "short term pain." It certainly merits research and potential action.

How to capture the savings:

Each time you pay your monthly cell phone bill, put $50 (or whatever you no longer pay for the land line) in your Freedom Jar. Deposit it into your Freedom Account – and do it each month! Track the progress on your Thermometer by filling in the appropriate level.

 FREEDOM WEAPON #13 – Quit Smoking

Estimated savings = $1,200-$1,800/year/ person –$2,400-$3,600/couple

A friend of ours who lived modestly in a mobile home park had a dream of buying a small fishing boat and motor. Despite his passion for fishing and deep desire for the boat, he saw no way financially to achieve it.

Then he saw a short TV news report on D-Day (National Day to Quit Smoking) that someone who smoked a $3.00 pack of cigarettes daily could save well over $1,000/year by quitting.

For the first time, he saw that his dream was possible. That very day he located his fishing and hunting magazine and cut out a picture of a small boat and motor. He placed the picture on his bedroom wall and put an empty fish aquarium beneath it. Beginning the next day, he quit smoking for the first time in 25 years.

Each day he put $3 cash in empty aquarium. At the end of each week, he deposited his $21 in a special savings account. In just over two years, he bought a used boat and motor that delighted him for many years.

I asked him how hard it was to quit.

"Gut wrenching," he replied. "At the beginning, I went through cold sweats, threw up and was a royal grump for the first month.

"But each time it would get bad, I would go in and look at the picture and the money in the aquarium – and I'd picture what it would be like to be sitting in that boat, living the dream.

"That picture was stronger than the temporary pain I was feeling."

Another example was a young couple in their late 20's who saw no way of paying off their credit card debt and little hope of savings and funds for retirement.

The husband said, "We finally realized the connection between a $10 per day smoking habit and the funds we needed to destroy our credit card debt and put money away for the future." (They each smoked a pack a day, which in their state was $5 per pack).

"We put a picture on our refrigerator of a senior citizen couple who were clearly living in poverty and poor health. Next to that, we put a picture of a senior couple who were in great health and enjoying their retirement years. Under these pictures, we put a sign that said, *Which do you choose?* This is right next to our Freedom Thermometer."

Every day, the husband and wife dropped $5 each into the Freedom Jar and, at the end of each week, deposited $70 into their Freedom Account. At $10 per day, it took them just over three months to establish a $1,000 Freedom Account. After two years, their credit card debt was gone and they are faithfully saving in their retirement account.

"Our future was literally going up in smoke," the husband said. "A $10 per day smoking habit was really hard to change – but with $3,650 per year saved by quitting, it was what we needed to turn our financial life around. As a side benefit, we have never felt better since we quit. It wasn't easy, but constantly looking at the pictures of the two senior citizen couples sure helped."

How to capture the savings:

After quitting, calculate whatever you currently spend on cigarettes per day, drop the savings at the end of each day into your Freedom Jar and record on the Freedom Thermometer as you deposit the total amount into your Freedom Account each week.

FREEDOM WEAPON #14 – Turning wine into savings

Estimated savings = $0-$3,000/year

A husband and wife, in their mid-30's, both worked at relatively high paying jobs. While they had no credit card debt, they also had no savings and nothing in their retirement account.

One day it occurred to them what a savings opportunity presented itself by just stopping drinking wine or mixed drinks when they went to a restaurant.

Their practice was to go to a sit-down restaurant at least twice a week and over the course of the evening to have 2 glasses of wine each.

As they calculated what they spent on the wine, they identified the average at $7 per glass (with tax and tip).

This couple's calculated savings:

2 glasses of wine @ $7 each = $14 x 2 people = $28/meal
$28/meal x 2 meals/week = $56
$56/week x 52 weeks = $2,912 annually

Within 18 weeks, after utilizing this Freedom Weapon, they had $1,000 in their Freedom Account. Soon, they were putting approximately $3,000 a year into retirement savings just from this Freedom Weapon alone.

How to capturing the savings:

After returning home from the restaurant, they would each deposit $14 into the Freedom Jar. At the end of the week, the savings were recorded on the Freedom Thermometer and deposited into the Freedom Account.

FREEDOM WEAPON #15 – Saving money on recreation and entertainment

Estimated savings = save $1,000 annually by tracking costs and being creative

Recreation and entertainment are wonderful things. The very word "re-creation" speaks to refreshment. Our bodies, minds and souls need time to revitalize.

This category of recreation and entertainment is amazingly diverse because of differences in individual tastes, time, income, age and even beliefs.

Generally speaking, recreation would include things like biking, swimming, camping, hiking, skiing, fishing, boating, golfing, broomball, Frisbee, horseshoes, dancing, and playing softball, baseball, football, basketball, hockey, soccer, etc.

Entertainment would include taking vacations and going to movies, concerts, football, basketball, baseball, hockey and soccer games, entertainment parks, state fairs, etc.

Spending on recreation and entertainment could be as small as $.99 to rent a movie to $20 to go to a movie and order popcorn, soda and candy.

It can be as small as paying $1 per hole to play golf on a municipal golf course, to paying tens of thousands for a country club golf membership. It can be as small as paying nothing to hear a free concert in the park – to $100+ per ticket for a big name entertainer.

So, with such a wide variance, how can we estimate savings – much less capture them?

First, go to your checkbook register and/or credit card bills for the last six months and add up what you spent in the areas you define as recreation and entertainment. Since cash is also used, estimate and add in what you may have spent at movies etc. where cash would normally be used.

Second, limit yourself to half your normal expenditure. Once you have determined what you spend, put a weekly limit on it. It will force your creativity to stretch it as far as you can. Plan your entertainment in advance so it's not just impulse.

A number of financial experts estimate that Americans spend 5-10% of their take home pay in this category.

For an individual or family whose take home pay is the national average of $2,500 per month that would mean an expenditure of $1,500-$3,000/year. That's approximately $125-$250 per month or $32.50-$65 per week.

If you and/or your family don't spend much on this area, move on. For others, however, this may be an opportunity to capture real savings – while still having great fun.

Third, by being creative and smart, enjoy all the fun you can while cutting your costs in half.

For instance, many people love going to movies. They also love movie theater popcorn, large sodas and candy to go with it.

At the time of this writing, movie tickets for adults are $10. To add popcorn, soda and candy will add $8-$12. So, the total cost is $18-$22.

How do some families cut the bill in half? The wife puts four candy bars from home in her purse, which they consumed during the movie (by the way, this is not illegal).

Was this a major sacrifice? No. Could they capture savings by being smart and creative? Absolutely!

Some theaters also charge less on certain days of the week and for matinees. Sometimes you can find coupons for movie theaters.

Some might say, "I could also save more in that scenario by renting a DVD and having popcorn at home."

Others have found ways to cut the costs at baseball, basketball, football and hockey games (especially major league). While they may not let you bring in a beverage, nothing stops you from bringing a treat in your pocket (it's not illegal). The cost of concessions at these events is massive because they have you for a number of hours as a captive audience. The goal is to get you to spend heavily on these high profit items.

Think. Be creative. Eat a big meal at home just before you go to the event.

Focus on lower cost recreation and entertainment. For instance, we love major league baseball, but started to go to minor league games. They were wonderfully entertaining and at half the cost.

EXAMPLES OF LOW COST RECREATION AND ENTERTAINMENT

Bicycling

Tennis

Volleyball

Ping Pong

Fishing

Horseshoes

Bowling

Softball

Hiking in state and national parks

Playing cards

Playing board games

Video games

Books

Free concerts

Library for movies, books and magazines

High school sporting events

Community concerts and theater

High school concerts and theater

Having people over for board games, cards, DVD, just talking

Church concerts, small groups and Bible study

Church softball, basketball, bowling, etc.

Company sports

How to capture the savings:

- Estimate your current weekly expenditure on recreation
- Set your goal to cut that in half by being creative and planful
- On the day you deposit into your Freedom Account, track your actual expenditure for the week and deposit the difference that you saved from the amount in #1. Then mark the amount on our Freedom Thermometer.

Want More Freedom Weapons?

If you would like to identify even more Freedom Weapons:

- Go to the internet search engines and look up Money Saving Tips
- Go to our website at www.thecreditcardtrap.com. There is a listing from readers of additional Freedom Weapons that have been helpful to them. By the way, feel free to write us about Freedom Weapons that you have successfully utilized and want to share with others.

GOING TO WAR – 7 STEPS TO VICTORY

Here is how to put the Freedom Weapons into action in your life:

Step 1 – Select the Weapon(s) that you feel would be the most effective for you.

Choose carefully because this really is your battle plan. If you are discussing it with a spouse and/or family – that is your war council. You are in this battle together.

Recommendations:

Choose 1 or 2 weapons to start with – no more! The reason for this is that when people try too many things, they usually lose focus and it becomes too difficult.

Choose something you know you can be successful with. You want to gain a series of small victories to achieve momentum. Think big, but start small.

What weapon or weapons did you choose?

1. _____

2. _____

Step 2 – Choose your starting date for your first week of battle and determine who is responsible for what.

Let's say John and Mary choose Freedom Weapon #3 (pack your own lunch) and Freedom Weapon #8 (shop rates for car insurance). They decide that beginning Monday of next week, they are both going to pack their lunches Monday – Friday before leaving for work. In their "war council," they discuss specifically what they want to have in those bag lunches. Mary volunteers to buy the necessary food at the grocery store next Saturday. Each is responsible to pack their own lunch daily.

John volunteers to research the various car insurance companies on Saturday and begin making calls on Monday during lunch. John and Mary hope to move quickly on this and make a decision by Friday.

They have selected their weapons and there is a clear strategy for the first week of battle.

Step 3 – Use the visuals for on-going motivation.

It may seem a little "corny" to drop a $5 bill into the Freedom Jar for each day that a lunch was packed, but most people say it is stunning to see how fast the jar fills up. Most feel there is a real sense of accomplishment at the end of the week when the cash is added up, progress marked on the Freedom Thermometer and the cash actually deposited into the Freedom Account. The feeling of progress and increasing momentum helps to keep motivation building – and turn good practices into a habit.

Step 4 – When the $1,000 Freedom Account level is reached – celebrate!

Before going to the next level, save for something you really need or want to buy. It might be a:

Dream weekend vacation	Dryer
Lawn mower	Cell phone
Laptop computer	Electronic game
Debt-free Christmas	Bicycle
Tennis, fishing, or golf equipment	

Next, put up a new thermometer with $300 marked at the top and a picture of what you want to buy. Then add one more Freedom Weapon to your strategy and use the same process you utilized to successfully put $1,000 into your Freedom Account (continue to use the Freedom Jar and weekly deposit).

When the $300 level is reached, withdraw the cash and enjoy the feeling of paying for your purchase only once – not 2, 5 or 16 times on a credit card.

This process will work for you over and over again. Save now, buy later!

Step 5 – Back to the Battle!

If you are NOT in credit card debt, the next battle is adding $1,500 to the Freedom Account on your way to the equivalent of 3 months take home pay.

Use the same process that brought you victory in the earlier steps. Put up a new thermometer with $1,500 at the top, use the Freedom Jar and weekly deposit.

As you contemplate your battle plan, review the Freedom Weapons and choose one more that you can add to the battle.

If you ARE in credit card debt – target the credit card that has the smallest balance. This is going to be a "search and destroy mission!"

Put up a new thermometer with the card's balance at the top. This is a "reverse process" as you use the marker to indicate the ever decreasing amount. Again, use the Freedom Jar, but at the end of the week make a payment against your card balance.

As you contemplate your battle plan, choose one more Freedom Weapon that you can add to the battle.

At minimum, these are the things that will spell victory:

- You are no longer using your credit cards, so you are no longer adding to the credit card balance.

- You are paying the credit card bill the day it arrives, so there is no chance of late fees added or bumping you into a higher interest rate (these can produce huge fees and even higher enslaving interest rates).

- You are paying at least DOUBLE the minimum payment – and continuing to pay that amount even when the required minimum goes down. For example, if you owed $2,000 and the minimum payment is $100 – at least pay $200 and keep paying $200, even when the next month's minimum payment is $95.

Step 6 – As each battle is won, move to the next – until the war is won

If you are NOT in credit card debt, the next battle is adding $2,000 to the Freedom Account on your way to the equivalent of three months take home pay – or beyond.

Use the same process that brought you victory in the earlier steps. Put up a new thermometer with $2,000 at the top, use the Freedom Jar and weekly deposit.

As you contemplate your battle plan, review the Freedom Weapons and choose one more that you can add to the battle.

As you start to see that victory is possible in achieving the second level of the Freedom Account, I would like you to dream a bit about things that will also become possible in the future using the same process:

- Debt-free vacations
- Debt-free Christmas
- Paying off all non-credit card debts
- Buying a car debt-free
- Paying off the mortgage on your house
- Building a retirement account and a college savings account – and having compound interest working for you!

For now, however, begin to picture yourself as a saver – because that's what you are.

If you ARE in credit card debt – target the credit card that has the next smallest balance. This is again going to be a "search and destroy mission!"

Put up a new thermometer with the card's balance at the top. This is a "reverse process" as you use the marker to indicate the ever decreasing amount. Again, use the Freedom Jar, and at the end of the week make a payment against your card balance.

As you contemplate your battle plan, choose one more Freedom Weapon that you can add to the battle.

When this battle is won, go to the next until all your credit card debt is gone.

After rejoicing, your next battle will be to build up your Freedom Account to the equivalent of three months take home pay – six months if you are over 45 years old.

Even though you are still in credit card debt, start to see yourself as a saver. And, in truth, if you have the first $1,000 in your Freedom Account, you are a saver!

I would encourage you to repeatedly say to yourself, "I am a saver and a conqueror, not a debtor and a slave. I will be free from all debt."

Words create powerful pictures in our minds – and we tend to fulfill the picture we set before us.

More about this in the next section. However, remember that you cannot hit a target that you cannot see.

Step 7 – Team up for the long haul

The war for Financial Freedom is a long-term struggle. It is won "one day at a time" by the seemingly small choices we make.

On-going motivation is very important. The Freedom Jar and Thermometer really help – keep using them. But sometimes the going gets tough and you need something more to keep going.

There is another powerful concept to consider called collective motivation or "teaming up." The Bible says it this way:

> Two people can accomplish more than twice as much as one. They get a better return on their labor. For if one person falls, the other can reach out and help. But people who are alone when they fall are in real trouble. A person standing alone can be attacked and defeated, but two can stand back to back and conquer. Three are even better, for a triple-braided cord is not easily broken. (Ecclesiastes 4:9, 10, 12 NLT)

At times your family can be that team – sharing the vision, helping in times of hardship, cheering each other on, and praying for one another.

There are also times when it is good to have friends to team with – people who share the same vision and goals. These are people you can meet with on a regular basis to discuss ideas, rejoice in each other's successes, help each other when the going gets tough – and to pray for each other on a regular basis.

This concept of collective motivation is what has made groups such as Weight Watchers, Alcoholics Anonymous, and numerous sports teams so successful over the long haul.

Some people combine this concept with Freedom Weapon # 9, the Freedom Meal. They get together with friends one evening a week for dinner. They make it a potluck with each family bringing salad and a hot dish or hot dish and dessert. They get a chance to fellowship, relax, laugh and find out how the week went for everyone (maybe even play some games after dinner).

They also substitute this evening for a night out at a formal restaurant and are able to put $10 savings per person in their Freedom Jar.

Regardless of how it's done, teaming up with others who share the same goals of getting out of debt and achieving financial freedom can be a powerful motivational help in achieving it.

The Impact of the Freedom Account on America

The funds you deposit in a federally insured credit union or small community bank, together with the savings of others, is called capital formation – and they drive a healthy, prospering economy.

These savings are vitally important not only for you and your family, but for America.

Most people ask, "How will my saving $1,000 or $7,500 or even $15,000 really impact America? My savings are so small compared to the needs of the nation."

When people unify in purpose, it's amazing what can happen. If the 85 million Americans who currently have no savings save $1,000 in a Freedom Account, what would that equal?

Answer: $85 billion!

If those 85 million Americans saved $7,500 in a Freedom Account, what would it equal?

Answer: $637.5 billion (that's over a half trillion)!

If those 85 million Americans saved $15,000, what would it equal?

Answer: $1.27 trillion!

That is $1.27 trillion of American savings – not money that the US government had to borrow from China to lend to our banks – but money that American citizens saved from "the grass roots up."

Would that have an impact on our communities and country? Absolutely!

Now, if the families who owe $1 trillion in credit card debt (at 16-35% interest) eliminate that debt and never carry credit card balances again – that's a swing of $2.27 trillion!

Too Idealistic?

You might be saying, "That's too idealistic. That will never happen."

That's what most of the world (and even many of the colonists) said at the beginning of the American Revolution. But with the power of a unified vision, a determined willingness to fight for freedom, and the help of Almighty God – the first American Revolution succeeded.

This one will too. How? One person, one family, one friend at a time.

Will you establish a Freedom Account? Will you encourage your friends to do the same? That formula is a key part of the battle plan for an American economic revolution from the grass roots up.

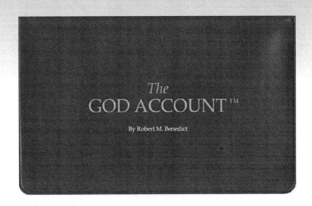

THE GOD ACCOUNT™

The God Account is another powerful tool that can transform your life, even as you change the world.

I speak from experience because the God Account concept has transformed my life, the life of my family, and the lives of many others who have also established God Accounts. We'll discuss more about this in the next section.

What is a God Account? In its first phase, it's a savings account dedicated to helping others in need.

Each week, as you deposit money into your Freedom Account, I am going to ask you to take 10% of the total and deposit it into this separate savings account called, The God Account – and only use those funds to help others in need.

It will help you see yourself as a giver and as a world changer – because that is what you will be if you utilize the concept.

What's your reaction?

Some people are immediately intrigued by this concept – others are more skeptical.

Both groups, however, tend to have the same three questions:

- How can giving 10% of my Freedom Account actually change the world?
- Won't giving away 10% slow down my progress on my way to financial freedom?
- Shouldn't I wait until I am out of debt to give to others in need?

Question #1: How can giving 10% of my Freedom Account actually change the world?

> If I accomplish the first level of $1,000 in my Freedom Account, 10% is only $100. Even at the second and third levels of the Freedom Account ($7,500 and $15,000 for the average American), 10% is only $750 or $1,500. How can that change the world?

Answer: It will change the world the only way the world is ever changed: one person, one family, one community at a time.

I recently reviewed the websites of a number of respected non-profit organizations to get some examples of the impact that $100 can have in helping people in need.

$100 can supply 500 pounds of rice and beans to starving families

Much of the developing world relies on rice and beans as a vital source of complex carbohydrates and protein.

Your $100 could provide 1,000 meals for badly malnourished families through the purchase of 500 lbs. of rice and beans.

$100 can provide a flock of 80 chickens

A flock of 80 baby chicks could help families with a sustainable source of protein from the eggs – as well as supplemental income from selling extra eggs.

Because chickens require little space and can thrive on available food scraps, families can make money without spending much. Chickens also help control insects and fertilize gardens.

Your $100 could supply four families with a starter flock of 20 chicks each.

$100 can pay for the shipping of $1,400 worth of donated medicines and medical supplies.

Every day, thousands of children die because they do not have access to basic medicines that could save their lives.

The impact of your $100 multiplies 14 times as you pay the shipping costs for donated pharmaceuticals and medical supplies such as: antibiotics, anti-fungals, anti-parasitic drugs, de-worming medications, disposable syringes, and urgently needed surgical supplies.

$100 can supply an entire family with clean water.

Household filters can mean the difference between life and death for people gathering water from dirty ponds, rivers and lakes.

Your $100 can supply a filtering unit that can provide clean, safe water through a natural process that removes pollutants.

Each family receiving a filter also participates in health and hygiene training sessions.

$100 can protect 10 children from dreaded malaria.

Malaria kills 1,000,000 people each year. Most who die of this treatable, preventable disease are children.

Your $100 will provide 10 children with mosquito bed nets and their family with malaria prevention education and access to malaria medical treatment for those struggling with the disease.

$100 can save one child from slavery.

Would it surprise you to learn that there are more slaves today than any other time in history? Today it goes by another name – human trafficking.

According to one organization, there are currently 27 million people trapped in this lifestyle. People are being sold, transported and used for profit. They are forced to beg, work in sweat shops, serve as child soldiers – or even as prostitutes. This respected organization has committed $1,000,000 to help with urgently needed shelter and vocational training.

Another well known non-profit successfully focuses on the slavery issue through:

Prevention – going into the villages where human traffickers target young children and providing food and other basic needs, removing one of the primary reasons that desperate families sell their girls and boys into slavery.

Direct outreach – ministering to young people on the streets who are forced to sell their bodies to survive, encouraging them with the good news of Christ and providing a new home where they can be protected and a vocation so they can break free of the sex industry.

This organization estimates the overall cost to rescue one child at just over $100.

$100 can be a significant "micro-loan" to help start a small business and break the poverty cycle.

There is an exciting concept called micro-lending where you can make loans (as small as $25) through non-profit organizations directly to people in underdeveloped nations who are trying to start small businesses as storekeepers, fisherman, farmers, etc.

Due to the screening, training and accountability structure of the non-profits who do this, over 98% of the loans are re-paid! It is one of the great success stories of the last 30 years in helping people break out of poverty. When the loan is repaid, you can lend it out to the next person – and then the next. The impact just keeps going.

With a number of these micro-loan organizations, you can actually see the pictures of the people who are requesting the loans and details of what they are trying to accomplish with their business. You also get on-going updates of repayments.

The Impact of the God Account in the United States

$100 may have significant impact overseas, but how can it possibly make a difference in America?

Gasoline for a single mom or dad

Let's say it's a weekend at the end of the month and you hear of a single mom or dad who doesn't have money enough to buy gasoline to get to work on Monday.

You get the funds from your God Account and you encourage that mom or dad by filling their tank.

Car battery for a college student

You hear of a college student away from home whose car battery died and they can't afford a new one.

You get the funds from your God Account and you take that student to the auto store and bless them with a new one.

Food for a soup kitchen or food shelf

There is an appeal at your church for the local food shelf that desperately needs to re-stock their supplies – or a soup kitchen that is nearly out of food.

You get the funds from your God Account and are amazed at how much food your $100 purchases (so is the food shelf or soup kitchen). Maybe you personally help distribute the food at the food shelf or serve at the soup kitchen. Perhaps you take your children with you to help buy or serve the food and teach them about giving and serving in the process.

Sleeping bags for the homeless

Your local newspaper carries a story about the homeless in your city who are in desperate need of sleeping bags to withstand the bitter cold winter nights.

You get the funds from your God Account and you not only buy three thermal sleeping bags, but you are able to personally give them to the three people whose temporal lives you may have even saved because of what you have done.

Encouragement for a pastor

You hear about the pastor of a small church who is overworked, underpaid, feeling unappreciated – and about to give up.

You take the money from your God Account (maybe baby-sit the children) and give this pastor and spouse a wonderful evening at a restaurant and movie, or a night away at a hotel. The pastor and spouse are refreshed because of what you did and are encouraged to keep going.

If you did these or other acts of kindness from your God Account (in the US or overseas), would you have made a difference in the lives of the people and families affected – even with a small amount of money?

Would the world be a better place because you live on the earth?

Giving Brings Happiness and Meaning

Giving to others not only changes the world of those who are helped, it transforms our world by the happiness and meaning it brings into our life. In fact, when we don't give and only focus on ourselves, our spirits begin to shrivel within us. We become depressed.

One of the great literary examples of this is the story of Ebenezer Scrooge in Charles Dickens' beloved novel, *The Christmas Carol.*

When Ebenezer was a miser, hoarding his riches, uncaring about others, and living in fear of losing his wealth – he was miserable.

But after a visit by three spirits on Christmas Day, he was given a second chance. Immediately he began to give to the poor and needy – and it transformed him! He came alive. He ran through the streets of London leaping for joy! He had never known such happiness in all his life.

Why is this? Because we were created to be givers and experience the happiness and meaning it brings.

Look at these verses:

> If you want to be happy, help those who are poor. (Proverbs 14:21 RB)

> Oh the joys of those who are kind to the poor. (Psalm 41:1 NLT)

> Jesus said: "You are far happier giving than getting." (Acts 20:35 The Message)

Does This Inspire You?

Does giving inspire you?

Would it give added motivation to you the next time you pack a bag lunch or order ice water rather than soda at a restaurant?

If yes, I invite you to go to Appendix #3 to read about the impact of giving at the next level, and the answers to the final two questions.

If not, move on to next section.

SUMMARY OF PART 2

AN AMERICAN REVOLUTION FROM THE GRASS ROOTS UP

RECOMMENDATION #1
SIGN YOUR OWN DECLARATION OF INDEPENDENCE
FROM CREDIT CARD DEBT – AND GO TO
WAR TO ACHIEVE IT!

RECOMMENDATION #2
ESTABLISH A FREEDOM ACCOUNT – TRANSFORM
YOUR FINANCES AS YOU CHANGE AMERICA

RECOMMENDATION #3
ESTABLISH A GOD ACCOUNT – TRANSFORM YOUR LIFE
AS YOU CHANGE THE WORLD

PART 3

LIVE YOUR LIFE
AS A SAVER
AND A GIVER – NOT
A DEBTOR AND
A SLAVE

*Harness the power
of the greatest economic
force on earth*

The 10-10-80 Battle Plan

HARNESS THE POWER OF THE GREATEST ECONOMIC FORCE ON EARTH

Your next battle is to harness the greatest economic force on earth and transform it into your greatest friend and ally. If you have ever had compounding interest working against you, you know its enormous power. Can you imagine having that power working on your behalf?

John Wesley, the founder of the Methodist Church, once said, "Earn all you can, save all you can, give all you can."

Wesley is not talking about an "out of balance, spend all your time and energy on the job, at the expense of all else" approach. He is talking about working diligently and using our God-given talents and gifts, so that our earnings are all they can be. In this quote, he is also focusing on the fact that we were created to be *savers and givers, not debtors and slaves.*

The Bible warns about debt in numerous places. Regarding savings, it says, "It is foolish to spend everything we make." (Proverbs 21:20b)

So, how do we best save, give – and harness the greatest financial force on earth?

Please Stop Here!

Before reading any further, however, I am going to ask you a favor. Please don't read any further in this section until you have:

- Destroyed all your credit card debt
- Established a Freedom Account with the equivalent of three months take home pay (six months if you are over 45)
- Faithfully used your God Account along the way

There are some very important and practical reasons why I am asking you to do that:

- By the time you reach those levels of success, you will be a battle-hardened conqueror who will look at the up-coming battle plan and say: "I can do that."

- You will already see the effectiveness of the Freedom Weapons. You will have made enough lifestyle changes that you already see yourself as a saver who is transforming your finances as you change America (because that's what you are!).

- If you have been faithfully using your God Account along the way, you will already see yourself as a giver who is transforming your life as you change the world (because that's what you are!).

However, if you have not yet gone through the battles and experienced the joy of hard fought victories, you will not yet have developed the discipline and strength to go to the next level.

You will not yet have the fully developed vision of yourself as a saver and a giver. If you can't see yourself free of credit card debt and having a fully funded Freedom Account, I'll guarantee that you will not be able to visualize yourself building wealth by harnessing the power of compounding interest.

You will look at the upcoming battle plan and say, "I can't do that."

So, please wait until you have become that battle-hardened conquer who has:

- Destroyed all your credit card debt
- Established a Freedom Account with the equivalent of three months take home pay (6 months if you are over 45)
- Faithfully used the God Account along the way

I look forward to the day of your return.

The Battle Plan For Success and Significance

Congratulations conquering warrior! You have already destroyed your credit card debt. You have met the enemy of compounding interest fighting against you, in one of its more formidable forms – and you have prevailed.

How much money each month did you formerly "pay the master," that is now free to be used "as you choose?"

You have successfully utilized a number of Freedom Weapons in your battles and have established new lifestyle habits that are producing savings each month. How much money each month do these savings equal?

You may gasp for a moment at the upcoming challenge, but as a battle-hardened conqueror, you will not stagger or turn back.

What lies ahead is the harnessing of the greatest financial force on earth, transforming it from one of your worst enemies to one of your greatest allies.

What lies ahead is great success and great significance.

10-10-80 BATTLE PLAN

When you get your paycheck, *before paying any bills:*

- Give the first 10% to God

  (Who uses this to change the world and transform your life – even as He helps you in very special ways)

- Give the second 10% to you

  (Who will build wealth, live debt free and harness the power of compounding interest)

- Live within your means on the remaining 80%

This is a battle plan that has brought success and significance to many people – enabling them to live as savers and givers, rather than debtors and slaves.

Remember the part of John Wesley's quote that said: "Save all you can, give all you can?" Let's review the battle plan, in that order, starting with "save all you can."

Live Your Life as a Saver – 10% deposited into savings BEFORE you pay any bills

Stories abound about people living on modest incomes who retire early with sizeable "nest eggs" and the freedom to do ministry, travel, start a second career or a business of their own.

Stories also abound about people living on modest incomes who, at the end of their lives, unexpectedly leave millions of dollars to charity.

Here is one example:

"Yesterday, the *LA Times* printed a story about an ex-teacher that left her fortune to her school district. They write, 'a woman (in Davison, MI) who spent 29 years as a teacher and counselor at the city high school has left $1.3 million to the school district.

'Edna Diehl left he money when she died at age 88 in July. The Davison Educational Foundation will hold the money in trust with the interest to be used to fund scholarships. The district expects the interest will generate about $60,000 per year, paying for two years worth of college for 5 students every year.'

"That's a generous gift that Mrs. Diehl left behind. What's even more remarkable is how a teacher amassed this amount of wealth on a teacher's salary and even after a long life of 88 years, had over $1 million left over to bequeath to her school district."[1]

How do these things happen? How do people accomplish this on modest incomes?

In most cases they learned a vitally important concept:

Small amounts of dollars, consistently saved over time, can produce huge results.

How? These people harnessed the greatest financial force on earth and transformed it from one of their worst enemies to one of their greatest friends. You can too!

Compounding Interest As Your Best Financial Friend

When our youngest son, Eric, was 23, he got a job that enabled him to save $50/week – if he so chose.

Eric was not willing to make the sacrifice necessary to save that $50 per week, unless he first understood what he would get in return. So let's do the calculation of what Eric's $50 per week could accomplish at a 5% interest rate.

$50/WEEK AT 5% INTEREST	
AT THE END OF YEAR	AMOUNT SAVED
1	$2720
2	$5527
3	$8477
4	$11,579
5	$14,840

After five years of weekly putting $50 into his credit union account at 5%, Eric would have nearly $15,000 for a down payment on a house – or whatever he might need at the time.

However, let's say that in five years, Eric doesn't need that $15,000 for a down payment. Let's say that at this point in his career, the $50/week habit is really no longer a sacrifice for him. Eric is excited to see what his ally, compounding interest, could do for him if he kept at it. Look at the incredible momentum the earnings pick up as time goes by.

AT THE END OF YEAR	AMOUNT SAVED
10	$33,828
20	$89,504
30	$181,278
40	$332,550
50	$581,896

Small amounts of dollars, consistently saved over time (using your powerful ally, compounding interest) can produce huge returns.

What if Eric could increase his rate of interest to 8% (which we'll discuss shortly)? What difference would that make to the total returns?

$50/WEEK AT 8% INTEREST	
AT THE END OF YEAR	AMOUNT SAVED
1	$2,763
2	$5,702
3	$8,885
4	$12,333
5	$16,069
10	$39,958
20	$128,720
30	$326,143
40	$765,246
50	$1,741,887

Over time, the difference of 3% is enormous. In fact, even the difference of 1% over time can be very substantial. However, everything starts with this vital concept:

Small amounts of dollars, consistently saved over time (using your powerful ally, compounding interest) can produce huge returns.

Let's take a look at the previous sentence in more detail.

Small Amounts Of Dollars...

Most big things in life that happen are the result of small things, done consistently, over time.

Some people get very excited about winning the lottery or a jackpot in Las Vegas. They visualize themselves getting that one big break that will solve all their financial problems and put them on "easy street" for the rest of their lives.

But the vast majority of people will never win the lottery. And the ironic thing is this: If the people who consistently invest in the lottery had invested those same amounts in savings, their ally, COMPOUNDING INTEREST, would have produced a remarkable jackpot on their behalf – guaranteed!

Think big, but start small. IT IS THE WAY OF LIFE. A grain farmer pictures a field with acres and acres of green corn stalks, beautifully tasseled, with each stalk bearing 5-10 ears of corn, each ear having a hundred or more kernels. But where does this great field of corn come from? Small seeds, patiently watered and tended to, that (over time) produce thousands of golden yellow kernels (seeds) for every one that was planted.

We live in Florida where vast groves of orange trees produce such abundant harvests of oranges that their branches strain under the weight. Where did these great orange trees come from? Small seeds, patiently watered and tended to, that (over the years) produce thousands and thousands of juicy oranges.

Whether it's corn, oranges, or our wealth – every great harvest starts with a small seed.

Your small seed might be $50 per week (like Eric) or it might be $100, or it might be $25 – but get started!

So many people think that a few dollars here and there don't matter. They do!

Regarding your wealth, think big (that's good), but start small. This is the way all great harvests happen.

The Bible puts it this way: "Don't despise these small beginnings." (Zechariah 4:10A NLT). The Bible also says: "Unless you are faithful in small matters, you won't be faithful in large ones." (Luke 16:10 NLT).

...Consistently Saved

We are creatures of habit. We each have good habits that serve us well and bad habits that hurt us. The more we can develop the good habits and eliminate the bad habits, the happier and more successful we will be.

One of the good habits my dad and grandfather modeled was consistent savings. I can still remember my father dressed in his blue and gray postal employee uniform, coming home each payday and (on a number of occasions) taking me to the bank.

He would hand me his paycheck and let me carefully hold it until we got to the bank. I still recall its light blue color, American eagle and United States of America emblazoned on it. It was very official.

Also, it wasn't printed on flimsy paper, but on a heavy card stock.

Even for someone as young as I was (5 or 6 years old), it was easy to tell what I was holding in my hand was very important – and I was about to be a part of a very significant transaction.

As my dad deposited his check, he would hand the teller his savings book and deposit slip so that 10% of his check went into his savings account – before the rest went into his checkbook.

Getting back into the car, he would show me the ever-growing amount in his savings account, and then say:

> If you pay yourself first by saving, you'll never miss it.
>
> Take care of your savings and one day it will take care of you.

His father had told him the same thing.

In the early years of their marriage, much of my parents' furniture was second hand or bought at a healthy discount because of a scratch or dent – or it was made by their own hands. They owned it debt free and it served the purpose just fine. *If they didn't have enough cash to pay for something, they didn't buy it* (in later years, they bought much nicer furniture – debt free).

My sister and I knew some families (most who made far more money than our dad) who always worried about money and were having their cars, furniture, TV's and even houses repossessed.

At times, we watched and heard husbands and wives in our neighborhood literally screaming at each other about money-related matters, while the kids cowered in fear. If a car suddenly needed a repair or a refrigerator or washing machine broke down, it was a major catastrophe – because they hadn't put money away for it and were living paycheck to paycheck.

That never happened at my parents' home. While postal employees did not make very much money in the 1950's, 60's and 70's, our family never missed a meal or a mortgage payment. We had nice clothes and my sister and I grew up in a loving, stable environment.

If a washing machine or refrigerator broke down and my dad couldn't fix it, it wasn't a catastrophe in our family. Dad just went to the bank and drew money out of the savings account that he consistently added to every payday.

Another endearing memory for me was going to the bank as an adult, and coincidently walking up behind my dad, who was in line with his paycheck. There he was (nearly 20 years later) with his savings book in his hand, paying himself before the other bills – while he and mom lived comfortably within their means.

It was a consistent, life-long habit that served my dad, grandfather and my own family exceedingly well. It will yours too!

Here's what God has to say about this:

Fools spend whatever they get. (Proverbs 21:20B NLT)

Lazy people should learn a lesson from the ants. They have no leader, but they store up their food during the nice days of summer, getting ready for the cold winter. (Proverbs 6:6-8 RB)

...Over Time (Using Your Powerful Ally, Compounding Interest), Can Produce Huge Returns

We've talked about starting with small amounts of money and consistently investing those small amounts over time. Now let's consider the final part of the sentence –

Notice again the graph showing Eric's investment of $50 per week at 5 and 8% compounded interest:

$50 SAVINGS PER WEEK		
AT THE END OF YEAR	EARNING AT 5%	EARNING AT 8%
1	$2,720	$2,763
2	$5,527	$5,702
3	$,8477	$8,885
4	$11,579	$12,333
5	$14,840	$16,069

AT THE END OF YEAR	EARNING AT 5%	EARNING AT 8%
10	$33,828	$39,958
20	$89,504	$128,720
30	$181,278	$326,143
40	$332,550	$765,246
50	$581,896	$1,741,887

While years 1-5 are impressive, look how the momentum picks up in years 10-20 due to the impact of compounding interest. Then look at years 20-30. More momentum! Look at years 30-40. Ever increasing momentum!

It's like a locomotive coming out of the train station, slowly at first, then picking up speed, then faster and faster – moving with such force that you would shudder at the idea of standing in its way.

Look at what an ally time is as it teams up with compounding interest. That's why it's important to start saving as early in life as possible (however, savings is helpful at any age – especially if you can maximize the rate of return and/or the amount of money you save).

The Impact of Your 10%

The battle plan calls for you to save 10% of your take home pay before paying any bills.

What would be the impact on your savings if you begin to do that now? Would it be worth the sacrifice?

Since the average American's take home pay at the time of this writing is approximately $2,500 per month, let's use 10% of that figure ($250) as the example (you can adjust upward or downward based on what 10% of your take home pay would be).

What is the impact of $250 per month being saved in a CD at your federally insured credit union (or community bank) at 5%?

$250/MONTH AT 5% INTEREST

AT THE END OF YEAR	AMOUNT SAVED
1	$3,345
5	$17,393
10	$39,394
20	$103,865
30	$210,049
40	$384,934
50	$672,973

Small amounts of dollars, consistently saved over time (using your powerful ally, compounding interest) can produce huge returns.

Now, let's say your $250 per month is invested in a healthy mix of mutual funds and long term CD's where you are able to boost your return to 8%.

$250/MONTH AT 8% INTEREST

AT THE END OF YEAR	AMOUNT SAVED
1	$3,404
5	$18,864
10	$46,596
20	$149,469
30	$377,808
40	$884,639
50	$2,009,621

The power of compounding interest is deeply affected by:

- Interest rates
- Amount of money invested
- The number of years invested

However, it all starts with this concept:

Small amounts of dollars, consistently saved over time (using your powerful ally, compounding interest) can produce huge returns.

How to Increase the Power of Compounding Interest Working for You

This book is not meant to be a course in financial planning.

Hopefully, this section will "whet your appetite" to do more research and take a course on financial planning.

However, here are a few tips as you consider ways to increase the power of compounding interest working for you.

ROTH IRA – TAX FREE INVESTMENT

$250/MONTH AT 5% INTEREST	
AT THE END OF YEAR	AMOUNT SAVED
1	$3,345
5	$17,393
10	$39,394
20	$103,865
30	$210,049
40	$384,934
50	$672,973

Take a look at the example of $250 per month at 5% interest and the amount that you would have after 10 years – $39,354.

That's a good thing, right? Right!

The one-year interest of 5% on $39,354 would bring you an additional $1,969.70. That's another good thing, right? Right!

It is, except that you will owe a fair amount of taxes on it. If you are in a 25% tax bracket, you will owe $492.43.

Moving forward 10 years, you will have $103,865 in your account. That's a good thing, Right? Absolutely!

The one year interest at 5% on $103,865 will bring you $5,193.25. That's a good thing, right? Yes, except if you are in a 25% tax bracket, you will owe the government $1,298.43.

Let's fast forward to 40 years. You will have $384,934. The one year at 5% interest would be $19,246.70 and you will owe the government $4,811.68 in taxes.

If you added up how much you paid in taxes over that 40 year period, can you imagine what the total would be? YOU DON'T HAVE TO!

If you put your savings into a ROTH IRA, the interest you earn will be TAX FREE.

Now, look at the impact on your account at 8%:

$250/MONTH AT 8% INTEREST

AT THE END OF YEAR	AMOUNT SAVED	INTEREST AT 8%	TAXES OWED W/O ROTH (25% Tax Bracket)	TAXES OWED W/ ROTH
10	$46,596	$3727.69	$931.92	$0
20	$149,469	$11,957.20	$2,989.38	$0
30	$377,808	$30,224.65	$7,556.16	$0
40	$884,639	$70,771.12	$17,692.78	$0
50	$2,009,621	$160,769.68	$40,192.42	$0

Some Facts About the ROTH

- The amount in your account will earn interest TAX FREE

- You can contribute up to $5,000 annually (less all contributions you might make to any other retirement plan) or $6,000 annually if you are age 50 or older

- You can withdraw the amount you contributed (not the interest) whenever you want, with no penalty. This flexibility can obviously be helpful if you are laid off work or at a time of increased expenses such as college tuition

- You can withdraw even some of the interest (up to $10,000) penalty free for such things as buying your first home

- For a single head of household, your adjusted gross income must be below $120,000 and for a married couple filing jointly, must be less than $177,000.

- You can make withdrawals of your interest with no penalty after age 59.5 provided the date you first started the plan was over five years previous

The contribution limits are for the year 2010

Traditional IRA, SEP, 401(k)

There are significant differences between the traditional IRA, SEP and 401(k) retirement plans and the ROTH retirement plan. While you will need to research and/or ask your financial adviser, here are a few key differences:

- What you contribute to these accounts is tax deductible. You are using pre-tax dollars rather than after-tax dollars.

  For instance, let's say you invest $250/month for 12 months = $3,000. It's now tax time. Unlike your contributions to the ROTH, you can deduct that $3,000 from your taxable income. If you are in a 25% tax bracket, calculate 25% of $3,000 = $750.

  You will pay $750 less in taxes. That's $750 that can be added to your savings when you get your refund, or help with your giving, or make an extra payment against the principle on your house or car – it's your option!

- The money you contribute to your traditional IRA, SEP, or 401(k) is tax deferred, not tax free.

  Unlike the ROTH, where the money you withdraw is tax free, you will pay taxes on the money you withdraw from these plans.

- There is less flexibility and there is a penalty for early withdrawals.

  Flexibility can either be good or bad. The harsher penalties for these plans can be good in the sense that there is a real incentive to use these savings for your retirement only – and find other ways to deal with lay-offs (the Freedom Account is a great example), or for helping with college tuition.

- While the limit you can contribute is the same for the ROTH IRA and the traditional or simple IRA, it is $16,500 for the 401(k) ($22,000 if you are 50 or older) and up to $49,000 if you have a SEP (these limits apply to the year 2010).

Compounding Interest at its Best

There are many companies that offer a match of your contribution to the company retirement program. These can range from $.50 for every $1 you contribute, to "dollar for dollar" up to a given amount of your gross salary.

The rates of return become astronomical, exploding the power of compounding interest!

Company Match of 50%

Let's continue to use the example of $250 per month. If you contributed that $250 to your retirement plan and your company provided a 50% match ($125), your monthly total becomes $375. Here is the impact of that extra $125 per month at 5% and 8%:

$250/MONTH vs $375/MONTH AT 5%		
AT THE END OF YEAR	$250/month	$375/month
1	$3,345	$4,624
5	$17,393	$25,609
10	$39,394	$58,473
20	$103,865	$154,780
30	$210,049	$313,397
40	$384.934	$574,642
50	$672,973	$1,004,914

$250/MONTH vs $375/MONTH AT 8%		
AT THE END OF YEAR	$250/month	$375/month
1	$3,404	$4,700
5	$18,864	$27,738
10	$46,596	$69,062
20	$149,469	$222,355
30	$377,808	$562,611
40	$884,639	$1,317,855
50	$2,009,621	$2,994,227

When your employer matches 50% of your contribution, you are making:

- An extra 50% on your money (where else can you make 50%?)
- 5% or 8% on both your contribution and your company's contribution
- The earnings on all this are still growing tax deferred
- You are still able to take your deduction of $3,000 off your taxable income ($250 per month x 12 months)

That is a powerful use of compounding interest!

What would the figures be if your employer matched your contribution dollar for dollar? They would obviously double the impact of your $250 per month investment. Take a look at it at 5% and 8%:

$250/MONTH vs $500/MONTH AT 5%

AT THE END OF YEAR	$250/month	$500/month
1	$3,345	$6,690
5	$17,393	$34,786
10	$39,394	$78,788
20	$103,865	$207,730
30	$210,049	$420,098
40	$384.934	$769,868
50	$672,973	$1,345,948

$250/MONTH vs $500/MONTH AT 8%

AT THE END OF YEAR	$250/month	$500/month
1	$3,404	$6,808
5	$18,864	$37,728
10	$46,596	$93,192
20	$149,469	$298,938
30	$377,808	$755,616
40	$884,639	$1,769,278
50	$2,009,621	$4,019,242

When your employers matches your investment dollar-for-dollar, that's an immediate 100% return! In addition, you are experiencing the stunning power of compounding interest on both your contribution and your company's – and it's working on a tax-deferred basis.

What an explosive combination!

Is there any reason you would not do this? The only reason would be if your company would only allow you to invest in their stock.

There is safety in diversification and most companies allow you to self-direct your savings into CD's, bonds and stocks (if you do stocks, mutual funds will help you diversify).

Where to Go From Here

Remember how this section started:

Stories abound about people living on modest incomes who retire early with sizeable "nest eggs" and the freedom to do ministry, travel, and start a second career or a business of their own.

Stories also abound about people living on modest incomes who, at the end of their lives, unexpectedly leave millions of dollars to charity.

How do these things happen? How do these people accomplish this on modest incomes?

After reading about the amazing impact of compounding interest, it's not hard to figure it out, is it? They knew this vitally important concept:

Small amounts of dollars, consistently saved over time, can produce huge results.

These people harnessed the greatest financial force on earth and transformed it from one of their worst enemies to one of their greatest friends. You can too!

Save 10% of Your Take Home Pay Before Paying Any Bills

What does 10% of your monthly take home pay equal? If you saved that amount each month and invested it at a reasonable rate, what would it equal in 5-10 years? How about 20-30 years. Or 40-50 years?

Does the long term gain outweigh the short term pain?

As I related earlier, when I was five or six years old, my father used to take me to the bank when he deposited his paycheck. As he deposited 10% of his pay into savings and showed me the ever growing amount in his bank book, he would say: "If you pay yourself first by saving, you'll never miss it."

At the time in Dad's life that he told me this, I am sure his statement was 100% true – he never missed it. He had done it for years as a habit and he and mom simply adjusted to live on what remained of his pay.

However, when Dad first started this practice (as his father did before him), I am sure there was a period of adjustment. My parents had to calculate their budget and figure out how to make it happen – because they were not going to spend more than they made. This "living within their means" was a cornerstone of their financial success – and the cornerstone of financial success for families living across America who practiced:

- Save now, buy later
- If you don't have the money for something, don't buy it
- Short term pain for long term gain
- Debt is serious and to be paid off ASAP
- Savings are essential, they bring financial freedom

How About You?

Are you willing to implement this part of the battle plan – 10% of your paycheck into savings, to help you live as a saver while harnessing the strongest financial force on earth on your behalf?

Can you visualize the impact on your family as the years go by? Can you visualize the impact on America if millions of our people did the same?

How will an American economic revolution happen from the grass roots up? One person, one family, one friend at a time.

It starts with <u>you</u>!

> **One of the primary things that separates those who have from those who have not is:**
>
> **The willingness to endure short term pain for long term gain.**

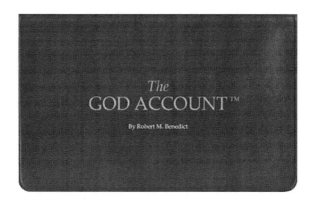

The
GOD ACCOUNT™

By Robert M. Benedict

LIVE YOUR LIFE AS A GIVER – 10% given to God BEFORE you pay any bills

When you give at this level, your God Account transfers from a dedicated savings account to a dedicated checkbook (it is much easier to give and keep track of your giving with a checkbook).

It's only an ordinary checkbook – but it has an extraordinary purpose. The money that goes into the account is deposited in a normal and natural manner – but what comes out of the account is powerfully supernatural and eternal in its impact.

The God Account is a dedicated checkbook that has the one and only purpose of housing the person's tithes and offerings (a tithe is 10% of one's income given back to God – offerings are whatever is given above the 10% tithe). Once the money is deposited in the God Account, the next step is to prayerfully ask God where He wants His money to go.

How the God Account Concept Began

Many years ago, I went through the failure of a business start-up venture that destroyed 10 years of savings. My wife, Pauline, and I were down to $28. Except for one illiquid investment, we were flat broke. In fact, we were worse than flat broke.

I had signed a very large company loan at the bank as a subsidiary guarantor – a loan that (after the company went out of existence) would take many years of my life to pay back.

There were also the thousands and thousands of dollars of company expenses on my personal credit card (that would never be reimbursed), accumulating interest at 18%. We had also financed our mortgage to the hilt in order to survive – resulting in huge monthly payments. Thousands of dollars in company debts were owed to local businesses that I felt a moral responsibility to somehow pay back – and they were constantly calling about payment.

Then there were the disappointed investors, some of whom were friends and relatives. In addition, I had a five-year-old son, a newborn son and a wife who were looking to me to provide for their needs. I also had no job.

I hardly slept. My blood pressure was so high that I would frequently get spontaneous nosebleeds – and I occasionally blacked out. Taking Tylenol for headaches throughout the day was a daily routine.

It was during this nightmarish era that God showed me a Bible verse that revolutionized my life and set in motion the creation of the God Account.

One evening in this nightmarish era, I was reading the Bible and came across Malachi 3:10-12:

> Bring the full tithes into the storehouse, that there might be food in my house; and thereby put me to the test, says the Lord of hosts, if I will not open the windows of heaven and pour down for you an overflowing blessing. I will rebuke the devourer for you so it will not destroy

the fruits of your soil; and your vine in the field shall not fail to bear, says the Lord of hosts. Then all nations will call you blessed, for you will be a land of delight. (RSV)

The verse took my breath away! I could hardly believe that it was actually saying what it was saying! Previously I had heard about tithing. I knew it meant giving 10% of one's income to God's work. *But this was God Himself challenging me to test Him* by giving Him the tithe and seeing if He would not open the very windows of heaven and pour me out an overflowing blessing. The part that really ministered to me was where God said He would rebuke the devourer for me and that my vine would not fail to bear.

It had been a long time since I had seen anything but losses. The devourer had destroyed my finances, health and peace. With everything inside me, I wanted the devourer in my life defeated. I wanted to start earning again, pay debts and see my family survive. From the pages of the Bible, *This was God Himself telling me how – He was showing me the way.*

There was an excitement that rose up inside me, blasting through the dazed fog of depression and defeatism that gripped my spirit. With more enthusiasm than I had had in a long time, I took the Bible over to my wife, Pauline, who was seated at the kitchen table. "Polly, you've got to read this! This is God Himself talking, telling us how to get out of this mess and how to prosper again. Read Malachi 3:10-12."

She read it and said, "What's a tithe?"

"It's 10% of our income," I explained. "God is saying that if we give Him 10%, He'll bless us, defeat Satan and that our vine will begin to bear fruit again. In other words, he will prosper us."

"There hasn't been any income, so 10% of nothing is still nothing," she said.

Now you have to understand that I was the one who got us into the venture where we lost nearly everything – so I didn't have a whole lot of credibility with her at this point.

After a pause, I said, "There's still $28 left in the savings account. This is God Himself challenging us to try Him out. In my heart of hearts, I believe Him. Let's give it to the church tomorrow."

"Jason needs shoes!" she pleaded.

"Pauline," I responded, "with the mountain of debts that we have and me without even a job, what do we have to lose?"

She rolled her eyes, shook her head, and said, "Go ahead, but I think you've totally lost it."

The next day I brought the $28 to the church. Of all the investments I have ever made in my life, it was the most precious – and it was the best.

Shortly after that, I decided to be self-employed doing what I had done earlier in my life – public speaking, training and consulting (sometimes there is a fine line between being self employed and unemployed).

God proved faithful to His promise. My vine indeed started to bear fruit again. It was not easy, but it was successful.

For two years, God worked one miracle after another as He stabilized us financially, healed me physically, gave us the gifts of sleep, peace and incredible spiritual adventure and growth.

Each month was a hair-raising, faith-building experience as to how God was going to help us meet our payments. Sometimes we got paid early for a seminar or speech that I did. Sometimes bills that should have arrived one month got delayed in their billing to the next month.

As the first of the month mortgage payment would loom on the horizon, Pauline and I would ask ourselves if we had done everything humanly possible on our part. If we could answer yes, we'd pray:

> God, your Word says that if we tithe, our vine will not fail to bear, you will rebuke Satan for us, and you will open the windows of Heaven and pour us out an overflowing blessing. Furthermore, you are the one who challenged us to put you to the test.

> We have tithed and we now lovingly and expectantly put you to the test. Thanks in advance for being faithful to your promise.

One memorable occasion occurred on the 28th of the month. We were well short of what we needed for the mortgage and had been praying fervently since the 20th. That night I got a call from a meeting planner who had heard me speak years before. He was in a desperate situation. He had lined up a keynote speaker for a convention in my hometown and now the keynote speaker was unable to attend. The speech was the next night, and he wanted to know if I could fill in.

I needed $800 more for the mortgage, so I told him if he could pay me $800 and pay me on the day of the speech, I would do it.

He said yes and I did too.

In those two years after we began to tithe (and later offerings above the tithe), we never missed a mortgage payment or any other payment. Our boys, as well as Pauline and I, never missed a meal (we weren't eating steak and lobster, but we never missed a meal).

In addition, Pauline saw God's faithfulness time and again on a monthly, weekly and even daily basis – and she went from skeptic to faith-filled believer.

Was it easy? I never worked so hard in my life. In fact, I prayed to God to make it easier. Instead, he made me stronger and increased my faith. He brought energy, health, joy and success. Amazingly, he even brought peace amidst the most trying experiences. There was no doubt about it. He was faithful to do what He said He would do. We were partnered with the Almighty, Creator God of the universe who happened to be our loving Heavenly Father as well.

Then, after two years of "just enough," God began to pour out overflowing financial blessings – which I'll tell about later.

The Impact of the Dedicated Account

As I stated earlier, after giving the first $28 to our church, God led us to put our future tithes and offerings into a separate checkbook that we called the God Account. Once deposited, this money was sacred, used only to help:

- Our church
- Ministries who were bringing people to Christ as they spread the Gospel.
- Ministries that were effective in helping those in need of food, clothing, housing, medical treatment, jobs, etc.
- Directly to people in need

Once deposited, it was now God's money and we would ask Him where He wanted His money to go. And, as I'll discuss in a moment, He consistently answered where He wanted it to go.

This concept of the money in the God Account truly being God's money, assured that there was no sense of loss as we gave – no feeling except the joy of being able to be a part of God's work in the life of others.

GOD REPLACES A BLOWN TIRE

Our oldest son, Jason, who was raised seeing the use of our God Account, established one of his own. When he was first married, he worked in the automotive department for Sears.

One cold, winter day a woman came into the store to replace a blown tire. When it came time to pay, she handed Jason a credit card that was rejected. After three more of her credit cards were rejected, it became apparent that she didn't have the money to pay for the tire.

Jason looked at the old car packed with small children and then excused himself to make a telephone call. He explained the situation to his wife and asked her thoughts about the situation and asked what she thought about using some of the money in their God Account to buy the new tire. She readily agreed and Jason told the woman who needed the tire, "There's no charge, ma'am. It's been taken care of."

The woman stood in stunned silence for a moment, then she exclaimed, "Thank God! Thank God! And God bless you!"

In her heart, that woman knew where the money was coming from – God. God had enabled Jason and his wife to play a part in showing God's mercy and love to that woman and her family.

I want to share Jason's comment about the God Account when he related the story to me. I also want to share that at this point in their lives, Jason and his wife were struggling financially. Jason said, "Dad, it's so easy and fun to give when you know it's God's money and not your own. When I paid for that tire, I felt no sense of loss, only joy." And, as his father, joy is what I felt as well.

Giving God the First Fruits

There was a second helpful concept that enabled the God Account to work for us as well.

In Proverbs 3: 9-10, God says: "Honor the Lord with your substance and with the *first fruits* of all your increase. So shall your barns be filled with plenty and your presses shall burst forth with new wine."

If we had received paychecks from a company on the first of the month, it would have been easier. We could have just calculated the 10% tithe and whatever offerings we wanted to give, written out the check to the God Account on the day we received the paycheck – then deposited on that day or the next day.

But I was self-employed. So, on the first of the month, I added up all the checks that I had received the previous month from my training seminars, speeches, and consulting (which was fairly easy at the beginning). Then I subtracted any costs such as the printing of workbooks, travel expenses, film rentals, or business office supplies or any business expenses I had incurred that previous month. From that sum, I calculated our 10% tithe before taxes (we were tithing on our pre-tax income). That very day we would deposit the tithe in the God Account.

As God stabilized us and prospered us, our percent of giving increased dramatically as we saw His faithfulness.

The concept of giving to God first before any bills were paid was a key factor in helping us to continue to tithe. I believe there are three reasons that God asks us to give to Him first:

You never have to go through the "gut wrenching decision" later in the month, deciding whether to give to God or pay your bills. It's already decided.

If you give to God first, He will help with the rest.

- You can watch it happen.
- Giving tithes and offerings first before paying any bills tests and grows your faith. In Malachi 3:10, God tells us to put Him to the test. At the same time, however, it also puts us to the test.
- We can talk about faith. We can study about it. We can pray for it. But ultimately we have to exercise it. Giving God's tithe first before paying any other bills is an act that requires us to exercise faith, not just talk about it.

THE GROWTH OF FAITH

For a period of time, tithing may force us to sacrifice something in the short term in order to see on-going long-term results. This initial time before our harvest comes in is a real faith-building period. Some people give up at this time rather than making the tithe a life-long commitment. As with any physical seed that is planted, the seeds of our giving take time to sprout, grow and produce a harvest. But ultimately God Himself assures us in Malachi 3:10-12 that "our vine will not fail to produce."

Later, as the "windows of heaven blessings" begin to flow, we see that God was faithful to His promise. As our faith grows, we start to give even a higher percentage. As a result, our harvest gets larger. Our faith grows stronger and we give even a greater percent. As a results, our harvest increases even more, etc. (by the way, these windows of heaven blessings are not limited to money).

In this process, our trust and faith in God grows even more and we start to exercise our faith in God's promises for other areas in addition to finances – believing that God will be faithful to those promises as well. Our excitement and love toward Him grow accordingly.

But the period at the beginning when we first begin to tithe is a definite "faith building" exercise.

God, Where Do You Want Your Money To Go?

When we first established our God Account and asked God in prayer where He wanted His money to go, both Pauline and I felt that we were to substantially increase our weekly giving to our church. It was interesting how that increase in giving helped us to feel even more a part of the congregation and its work.

Special Needs

Our church did a good job of bringing special needs before the congregation. Some months it was food for a food shelf or soup kitchen that was providing badly needed help to the poor. Other months it was an organization asking for clothing and school supplies for needy children about to go back to school or clothing for people trying to get a job but who couldn't afford clothing for the job interview.

As these speakers addressed the congregation, I'd look at Pauline, she'd look at me and we'd smile at each other – both knowing by the nudge in our hearts and spirit that this was for us. This was God telling us one of the areas He wanted His money to go to.

It's difficult to describe the joy we felt as we'd take the God Account checkbook, load the kids into the car, and head to the grocery store. We'd stock the grocery cart with canned hams and chicken, beef stew, chili, baked beans, lasagna, multiple kinds of soups, toothpaste, toothbrushes, and whatever else was on the list of needs given to us.

The grocery carts would be heaped with food – and we were always amazed at how little it would cost compared to what we thought it would cost. When the cashier announced the total, we'd write the check out of the God Account.

At the time, things were extremely tight for us financially. We were very, very careful what we bought. In fact, for two years, we did not go out to eat at a restaurant (not even fast food). Pauline really knew how to stretch a food dollar and make the food taste great.

Had we not had the God Account, would we have been asking: "Why are we doing this for others when we ourselves are struggling?"

Had we not put our tithes and offerings into the God Account before paying our bills, would we have had money in the God Account to buy the food?

Only God knows the answer to the above questions, but we *did* put the tithe in first and we did have the money and, because God answered where He wanted His money used, we *felt nothing but joy* as we unloaded bag after bag of groceries at the church. We were involved in God's work – and it felt great!

The same was true as we went to buy clothing and school supplies for needy kids who were about to go back to school as well as for people who needed dress clothes for a job interview.

Without a God Account, we may have been saying: "Hey, we're having trouble buying clothes and school supplies for our own kids. Plus, I need a new suit and Pauline needs new shoes."

With a God Account, it wasn't our money anyway – it was God's. We had an absolutely great time spending God's money to buy the clothes and school supplies He wanted us to buy. Our kids joined us in the shopping and had a wonderful time selecting what clothes to buy for each age group. When the sales clerk announced the total, I took out the God Account checkbook and paid the total with no sense of loss. It was God's money and we had the privilege of being a part of where He wanted His money to go. All we felt was pure joy.

Did God enable us to have food and clothing for our needs after we gave food and clothing to others? Yes He did – and we didn't have to go into debt to get them. They weren't designer clothes, but they were very nice. In fact, time and again we would find them on sale.

Other Opportunities

I want to be clear that we didn't give to every need that came up. Sometimes Pauline and I would pray about it and it was evident that a particular need was not for us, but oh the joy we felt when it was for us.

As time went on, we had a chance to help with members of our youth groups who were going on outreach tours or adults going on short-term mission trips. Outside our church, friends and acquaintances began to introduce us to people who were missionaries with Campus Crusade for Christ or Youth With a Mission – people who needed financial help to continue bringing the Good News of Jesus Christ to people across the world. In addition to these, we were also introduced to many small, but vibrant ministries that were having a mighty impact in the US and overseas, but operating on very small budgets.

Small as our God Account was, it was helping us to partner with and meet the needs of people in many areas who were carrying out the Great Commission and caring for the poor. We had asked where He wanted His money used – and He was answering!

Deep Meaning As God Continues To Answer

Like many churches, ours was many times behind in its budget. If anything new were to be done, the congregation would need to hold a fund-raiser or bring it before the congregation for a special offering. One Sunday, someone mentioned that there were a number of young families (like ours) who wanted the church to sponsor a film series on marriage and raising children. Christian psychologist, James Dobson, produced this particular series. The problem was the $350 (1984 pricing) needed for the film rental, shipping and limited advertising. Pauline and I looked at each other and determined to go home and see how much money was in the God Account.

We had exactly what was needed and after receiving the check from our God Account, our excellent pastor took care of the rest.

On the first of 4 nights, over 100 people attended. The next week, the crowd was even larger as people told each other about how helpful the previous week's film had been. By the last week, we didn't have enough chairs to accommodate everyone who came – many from outside our church.

How do I describe the feelings of meaning that Pauline and I felt as we watched those hundreds of people get blessed by Dr. Dobson's God-inspired insight? God had given us the privilege of being a part of ministering to His people.

If we had not had the God Account we may have been complaining about the church and why they couldn't afford the film series. But with the God Account, we were constantly looking for where God wanted His money used and overjoyed because He was showing us.

Becoming a Peacemaker

A few months later, God again gave us an opportunity to play a role through the God Account in a little different manner. There was a dear friend of ours who was miserable because his former business partner wouldn't pay back $500 that was owed to him. He continued to ask for prayer at our Bible study group for two reasons:

- He needed the money
- He was emotionally drained due to the anger over the situation

Pauline and I prayed long and hard about the situation and finally felt a strong sense that God wanted us to play a peacemaker role. I called our friend and told him that God had made it clear to Pauline and me that, if our friend agreed, He wanted us to play a role in restoring the relationship between him and his former partner. I told him that we were to give him $500 from our God Account and settle the debt on behalf of his friend.

At first he objected strenuously, but when I described what the God Account really was and that it wasn't our money anyway, and related what God had told us in prayer – he finally agreed.

He gave a phone call to his former partner and told him that someone had paid the $500 debt. He also invited him to lunch and mentioned that I would be there as well.

On the day of the luncheon, I explained about the God Account and what God had told Pauline and me and that his debt was settled. He was stunned. "What do I have to do?" he asked. "Accept it," I said. "Receive it as God's gift to you. If someday you can help someone out, do it in Jesus' name."

The whole tone of the luncheon changed. He started apologizing to my friend who graciously forgave him and in a period of an hour they were sharing stories of past things they had done together, laughing and enjoying each other's company.

Our friend told me what a blessing that time was – both the money and being set free emotionally. His former partner walked away from that meeting set free from the debt and the feelings of division between him and our friend.

When I related the story of the luncheon to Pauline, however, we knew who felt the most blessed. Through the God Account we had been given the privilege to play the role of being peacemakers.

Question: If we hadn't decided to tithe and give offerings, if we hadn't established a God Account, if we hadn't asked God where He wanted His money to go, would we have been given such a privilege?

Question: If we had been given the privilege, but hadn't had a God Account, would we have responded?

27 Years Later

In the 27 years following the events that I have been describing, God has vastly expanded the success of my business.

He led me to focus on teaching negotiations to people involved in purchasing and sales. He has blessed my company and enabled me to teach my seminars at some of the largest corporations in the world.

After eleven years of working entirely by myself, the level of my business grew to the point where I needed to train another trainer to do what I do. Two years later I had to add another trainer – and then another. These trainers have greatly multiplied my impact (as well as tithes and offerings) as they have taught my courses in Europe, Asia and South America as well as across North America.

I want to make this point very clear: The success of my business has not been because of my great wisdom or skills in selling or marketing. At best, I am an average salesman. *But God has provided astounding sales!*

I am a pretty good public speaker, but God has given me something of significant value to teach in my courses.

God expects me to do my part, to work my hardest, and to give my very best. He will not honor it unless I do. But, He is the one who has faithfully poured out an overflowing blessing – just as He promised to do in Malachi 3:10-12 to *anyone* who will trust Him with tithes and offerings.

As a result of God's faithfulness (and He is faithful!), the amounts we give today from our God Account have vastly increased.

We have been given the privilege of playing significant roles with ministries worldwide in spreading the Gospel, helping people in need, and supporting multiple churches.

The amazing thing is that Pauline and I did not purposefully set out to be involved in ministries across the United States or in Nigeria, Russia, China, India, Indonesia, Peru, Argentina, Brazil, Jamaica, Haiti – or any of the countries God has led us to.

Even so, over the last 27 years, our home has been honored with the presence of missionaries, pastors, and lay workers from around the world. These are people we have partnered with financially and people who we continually pray for (and they pray for us!).

In not one case did we say, "we want to minister in these countries." Yet over the years, God brought their needs to our attention and gave us the privilege (and it is a privilege) to play a role.

There is hardly a week that goes by that we don't receive an e-mail, letter, phone call, or DVD updating us on what the various ministries we support are experiencing. Sometimes they relate great stories of what God is doing. It might be souls won and discipled for Christ, or great progress in feeding the hungry, providing clean water, clothing, housing, or meeting medical needs. We rejoice with them as full partners.

Sometimes they relate an urgent prayer request that they want us to pray about. Sometimes it is us sending them urgent prayer requests that we need prayer for. Sometimes Pauline and I personally go to see what is happening on the ministry front and to help our partners.

Our partnership with these ministries has become a treasured focus of our life. Certainly Jesus is correct when He says, "Where your treasure is, there will your heart be also."

Actually, God has transformed the focus of our life through giving. He has brought deep meaning, prosperity here on the earth, and His promise of rewards in eternity.

However, lest you think we are so saintly, let me remind you of our motivation when we began to tithe 27 years ago.

It had little to do with wanting to be more obedient to God or to grow in faith or to show our deep love and thankfulness for His gift of eternal life. We were not "on fire" to spread the Gospel, help the poor, or support the church – that came later in the transformation process. Truthfully, we were one step from bankruptcy. We had tried everything else, why not try tithing? If tithing didn't work and God wasn't faithful to His promise in Malachi 3:10-12, we were done.

I am a former mayor of Minnesota's fourth largest city, a former state senator, a former divisional general manager and corporate vice president of a nationally known computer company, and for over a quarter of a century, I have made my living teaching contract negotiations to some of the largest corporations in the world. I do not look at the world through rose-colored glasses.

27 years ago, God challenged my wife and I to put Him to the test (His words, not mine) in Malachi 3:10-12. 27 years later, I am categorically saying, that *God is faithful and that His challenge to us in Malachi 3:10-12 can be trusted.* I am saying that to those who take Him up on His challenge and continue to give tithes and offerings as a way of life, God will transform your life even as He grows your faith. Your faith will strengthen and then soar as you watch Him work.

Do you know what else will grow and strengthen? Your love for God. You'll want to spend more time with Him. There will be a desire in your heart to learn more about Him through His Word.

The Greatest Story is Yet to be Written – Your Story

I get so excited when I start to relate what God has done in my life that people think I am a minister rather than a businessman. Sometimes I can't help myself, the stories of God's faithfulness just keep flowing out. *But the greatest story has yet to be written – your story!* You can't even imagine the wonderful things that God will do through you as you trust Him with your tithes and offerings. There are people in desperate need throughout the world that will be fed, clothed, housed, educated, healed, given hope because of your decision.

There are people who you will meet in heaven who will be saved for eternity because of your decision.

If you give tithes and offerings, asking God where He wants His money to go, He will give you stories of deep personal meaning and miraculous happenings – stories that will be passed down through the generations of your family and be remembered by God forever.

Then, as you watch God give back and prosper you on the earth, He will build your faith. As a bottom line businessman, my position is: If I can't trust God for the things He says about this world, how can I trust Him about the things of the next world?

Remarkably, God has also promised to reward every act of kindness done on His behalf – *forever.*

Let me end as I started: The God Account is only an ordinary checkbook – but it has an extraordinary purpose. The money that goes into the account is deposited in a normal and natural manner – but what comes out of the account is powerfully supernatural and eternal in its impact.

The key, of course, is tithes and offerings – God's plan for giving and receiving. But the use of a separate, dedicated God Account has been a practical and marvelous help to myself and family in being set free to fully experience the joy of giving. Our hope is that it will be a help to you and your family as well.

How About You?

Are you willing to implement this part of the battle plan – 10% of your income given to God?

Can you visualize the deep impact on you and your family?

Are you ready to transform your life and change the world in the process?

How will the world be changed? One person, one family, one community at a time.

It starts with *you*!

The Battle Plan For Success and Significance

10-10-80 BATTLE PLAN

When you get your paycheck, before paying any bills:

- Give the first 10% to God
  (Who uses this to change the world and transform your life – even as He helps you in very special ways)

- Give the second 10% to you
  (Who will build wealth, live debt free and harness the power of compounding interest)

- Live within your means on the remaining 80%

This is a battle plan that has brought success and significance to many people – enabling them to live as savers and givers, rather than debtors and slaves.

[1] Posted by Nina at www.queercents.com/2006/09/11

ABOUT THE AUTHOR

Robert Benedict was elected mayor of Minnesota's 4th largest city (Bloomington) at age 23. Two years later he was re-elected by the largest majority in the city's history. At age 26 he was elected as one of the youngest members of the Minnesota State Senate.

At 29, he was hired as a divisional general manager for National Computer Systems and at age 30 (after not seeking re-election to the Senate), was named a corporate vice president.

At age 32 Benedict left NCS to head a "start up" venture that utterly failed, devastating Benedict's finances and health. In addition, he was a subsidiary guarantor of the company's large bank loan that would take him many, many years to pay back.

After the company's demise, he was also left with thousands of dollars of company debt on his personal credit card (which also took years to pay off). Benedict gained first hand insights into high credit card rates, debt, and the enslaving power of compounding interest working against him.

It was during this time of despair that God powerfully moved in his life with physical, emotional and financial healing as well as much spiritual teaching.

At the depth of this situation, Benedict and his wife, Pauline, read Malachi 3:10-12 about tithes and offerings. They established a special "God Account" checkbook and at the first of each month deposited their tithes and offerings – asking God in prayer where He wanted His money to be given.

Since 1984, Benedict has been the president of Benedict Negotiating Seminars Inc., teaching his negotiation seminars to some of the largest companies in the world. He has also taught other trainers how to implement his course and they teach his seminar not only in North America, but in Europe, South America and Asia as well.

Benedict is also chairman of the board of the Institute for Economic Freedom, a non-profit organization dedicated to helping Americans break free of credit card debt.

He and his wife are the parents of two adult sons, Jason and Eric, and one granddaughter, Savannah.

APPENDIX #1

The Credit Card Act of 2009

In 2009, the US Congress passed The Credit Card Act to deal with some of the most insidious behaviors of the credit card industry toward the American people.

Some of the areas included:

Fairer payment allocation

In the past, credit card companies would apply above-the-minimum payments to the lower rate balances first (this enabled them to keep the customer in debt longer and at a higher interest rate). Under the new law, the above-the-minimum payment must apply to the highest interest rate.

Ends double-cycle billing

The new law bans double cycle billing, the practice of basing finance charges on the current and previous balance. Under this method, the issuer would charge interest on debt already paid off the previous month (devious seems too kind of an adjective to describe this practice)!

More time to pay

Credit card companies must send out statements 21 days before a payment is due rather than 14 (pay it the day it arrives!).

Restricts issuance to young people

Consumers under age 21 who can't prove an independent means of income or provide the signature of a co-signer age 21 or older, cannot be approved for a credit card.

According to a recent Sally Mae Study, college students carried an average balance of $3,173 on their credit cards in 2009 – a record high.

An amazing 82% revolved the balance each month.

While the new law will not stop the industry from targeting our young people, it at least slows them down.

Informing customers about the impact of the minimum payment

As I mentioned earlier, for the first time in 30 years, the credit card companies will have to reveal on the statement:

- How long it will take to pay off the balance if a customer only makes a minimum payment.

- How much the customer would need to pay monthly to pay off the balance in three years.

APPENDIX #2

Question and Answer on Small Community Banks
(taken from Riverpost Reporter, By Fritz Mayer)

Question: How can I locate a highly rated community bank?

Answer: In connection with the movement to move money, the website, www.moveyourmoney.info was created where consumers can enter their zip codes and find highly rated community banks in their neighborhoods.

Questions and Answers on Credit Unions
(taken from Frontline®, The Card Game, By Jonathan Jones and Zachary Stauffer)

Question: Who can join?

Answer: By law, every credit union has a specifically defined field of membership. Each one serves members who have a "common bond" which could include employment, geographic location, schooling, or military service. If you don't fall into an obvious category, but a member of your family does and is a member of a credit union, chances are, you can join the same one. Proponents say, with 92 million credit union members nationwide and some 8,000 institutions to choose from, with a little research, almost everyone can find a credit union that they are able to join.

Question: How do I join?

Answer: If you employer doesn't offer membership in one, you can find a credit union through Online Locators or www. findacreditunion.com. The Credit Union National Association (CUNA) can also put you in touch with your credit union state league (leagues are credit union trade associations) by phone at 800-358-5170 or online. Not all credit unions are the same so it's important to research the specific services they offer. At larger credit unions you will find virtually all the same services that banks have.

Question: Are savings accounts insured?

Answer: Since 1970, credit unions have been insured by the NCUA and are backed by the full faith and credit of the US government. The administration's insurance fund works in the same way as FDIC insurance does for banks – accounts are guaranteed for $250,000. Almost all of the 8,000 state and federally charged credit unions are insured by the fund, with the exception of a few that have elected to have private insurance. Make certain you research your credit union as to how they are insured.

One more question about credit unions:
(taken from Daniela Perdomo,@ www.alternet.org,
"Fury at Wall Street Banks Fuels Public Action
for Move Your Money Campaign."

Question: What is the American Debt Relief Challenge?

Answer: The American Debt Relief Challenge, which aims to get people to transfer their credit card balances from big banks to credit unions, shows that Americans have saved nearly $20 million by transferring. That's a monthly average of $200 in savings per customer, says Jamie Chase, a principal at Credit Union Strategic Planning.

www.ADRChallenge.com is another website that will list credit unions that can help you move high interest rate big bank credit card balances to much lower credit union rates.

APPENDIX #3

GOING TO THE NEXT LEVEL

Let's dream for a moment about giving at the next level.

Visualize the impact of $750 in the God Account or $1,500 (10% of the next levels in the Freedom Account for the average American).

Sponsoring Children

For $750 you could sponsor two children for an entire year (or four children for $1,500). This means their food, shelter, clothing, education and medical needs completely taken care of by your giving.

Would that make a difference in the lives of those children? Talk about changing the world one child at a time!

Would having their pictures and letters on your refrigerator next to your Freedom Thermometer have an impact on seeing yourself as a giver – as a world changer?

Would it give added motivation to you the next time you prepare a Freedom Meal at home or watch the standard cable TV package vs. the expanded number of channels?

Sponsoring Native Missionaries

For $750, you could sponsor two full time native missionaries for an entire year and play a foundational role in every life that was changed for eternity.

Chickens, Chickens Everywhere

We just mentioned putting pictures of sponsored children on your refrigerator. Let's try it with the example of providing families with baby chicks.

At $750, you would be putting up a picture of 600 chickens, providing 30 families with starter flocks of 20 chickens each. At $1,500 you would need a wide angle lens to photograph 1,200 chickens providing 60 families with a starter flock of 20 chicks. Can you imagine the difference in the quality of life in those families?

Talk about changing the world one family at a time!

Malaria Nets for an Entire Village

$750 would supply 75 malaria bed nets and $1,500 could supply 150 – enough to protect an entire village from that dreaded disease.

Would your giving have made a difference to those people?

Talk about changing the world one community at a time!

THE IMPACT OF THE GOD ACCOUNT
IN THE UNITED STATES

A Neighbor keeps their home

A neighbor whose company laid them off is going to lose their home, but you go to your God Account and the $750 or $1,500 pays their mortgage payment.

Church programs that won't be cut

Your church's giving is down and a key youth program or senior citizen program is going to have to be cut – but you go to your God Account and the $750 or $1,500 restores a key outreach effort.

Or, your church's giving is down and they are forced to cut back their support of vital missionary and evangelistic efforts – but you go to your God Account and your $750 or $1,500 inspires others to give as well. The programs are fully funded and the eternal destiny of many people is changed forever – due in part to your giving.

Family keeps their children

You hear about a family in the poverty stricken areas of Appalachia who are going to lose their children to social services because they can't afford to repair their home. You go to your God Account and the $750 or $1,500 pays for the roofing materials that volunteers will use to repair the roof (maybe you actually go there and help in the repair).

A family is kept together because of what you did.

Radio and TV Ministries for Shut-Ins

There are radio and TV ministries that inspire and minister to people who are shut in and can't go to church. The gift from your God Account helps keep those programs on the air, blessing people who are homebound.

Prison Ministries

There is a prison ministry that provides Christmas gifts to children of prisoners and they are many gifts short of the need.

There is another prison ministry that God is using powerfully to bring salvation to inmates and establish the lowest rate of return to prison after release anywhere in the nation. The ministry is in desperate need of funding to continue.

In each case, you go to your God Account and your $750-$1,500 is a God-send that helps keep them going.

If you did these, or other acts of kindness from your God Account (in the US or overseas), would you have made a difference in the lives of the people, families and communities affected?

Would the world be a better place because you lived on the earth?

Question #2: Won't giving away 10% slow down my progress on my way to Financial Freedom?

Answer: In the short term, yes. But the benefits in happiness, meaning and motivation will more than make up for it. In the long term, no. It will speed up your progress.

Take a look at these Bible verses:

> Give and it will be given to you. A good measure, pressed down, shaken together, and running over will be poured into your lap. For with the measure you use, it will be measured to you. (Luke 6:38 NIV)

> A generous person will prosper. He who refreshes others will themselves be refreshed. (Proverbs 11:25 NIV)

> If you help the poor, you are lending to the Lord – and He will repay you. (Proverbs 19:17 NLT)

As you read those verses, does it sound to you like what we bring into the lives of others comes back into our own?

Does it sound like God Himself is encouraging us to give and then gets involved in a special way to help those who give?

Take a look at the following verses:

> Remember this – a farmer who plants only a few seeds will get a small crop. But the one who plants generously will get a generous crop. You must each make up your own mind as to how much you should give. Don't give reluctantly or in response to pressure. For God loves the person who gives cheerfully.
>
> And God will generously provide all you need. Then you will always have everything you need and plenty left over to share with others.
>
> As the scriptures say: "Godly people give generously to the poor. Their good deeds will never be forgotten."
>
> For God is the one who gives seed to the farmer and then bread to eat. In the same way, He will give you many opportunities to do good and He will produce a great harvest of generosity in you.
>
> Yes, you will be enriched so that you can give even more generously. (2 Corinthians 9:6-11 NLT)

God has a plan that won't slow us down when we give – but actually speeds us on our way toward financial freedom, as He personally gets involved.

The plan is to prosper people who give so that they have what they need (without debt!) – and "plenty left over to share with others.

Interestingly, it also says He will give you many opportunities to do good. As we think and pray about how to use the money in the God Account, it is God who will bring the opportunities before us.

All these things and more I found to be true at a critical time in my life, when my finances had been devastated and my health and family were in great peril.

Question #3: Shouldn't I wait until I am out of debt to give to others in need?

Answer: No! Don't wait to give! I was deeply in debt when God used the concept of giving to help my family survive and stabilize – then thrive and prosper. He can do it for you too.

The God Account is a powerful tool that can transform your life with motivation, happiness and significance – even as you change the world one person, one family, one community at a time.

> When I was hungry, you gave me something to eat.
> When I was thirsty, you gave me something to drink.
> When I was a stranger, you welcomed me.
> When I was naked, you gave me clothes to wear.
> When I was sick, you took care of me.
> When I was in jail, you visited me.

> Then the ones who pleased the Lord will ask: "When did we give you something to eat or drink? When did we welcome you as a stranger or give you clothes to wear, or visit you while you were sick or in jail?"

> The King will answer: "Whenever you did it for any of my people, no matter how unimportant they seemed, you did it for me." (Matthew 25:35-40 Contemporary English Version)

For additional copies of

THE CREDIT CARD *TRAP!*
WHAT YOU DON'T KNOW <u>WILL</u> COST YOU

go to <u>www.thecreditcardtrap.com</u>.